Silver Burdett & Ginn
PENNSYLVANIA YESTERDAY AND TODAY

WILLIAM J. SWITALA, Supervisor of Social Studies and Foreign Languages, Bethel Park School District, Bethel Park, Pennsylvania

CONSULTANT

Howard A. Ohline, Professor of History,
Temple University, Philadelphia, Pennsylvania

SILVER BURDETT & GINN
MORRISTOWN, NJ • NEEDHAM, MA
Atlanta, GA • Cincinnati, OH • Dallas, TX • Menlo Park, CA • Deerfield, IL

SERIES AUTHORS

Val E. Arnsdorf, Professor,
   College of Education, University of Delaware,
   Newark, Delaware

Herbert J. Bass, Professor of History,
   Temple University, Philadelphia, Pennsylvania

Carolyn S. Brown, Late Principal,
   Robertson Academy School, Nashville, Tennessee

Richard C. Brown, Former Professor of History,
   State University of New York College at Buffalo

Patricia T. Caro, Assistant Professor of Geography,
   University of Oregon, Eugene, Oregon

Kenneth S. Cooper, Professor of History, Emeritus,
   George Peabody College for Teachers, Vanderbilt
   University, Nashville, Tennessee

Gary S. Elbow, Professor of Geography,
   Texas Tech University, Lubbock, Texas

Alvis T. Harthern, Professor of Early Childhood
   Education,
   West Georgia College, Carrollton, Georgia

Timothy M. Helmus, Social Studies Instructor,
   City Middle and High School, Grand Rapids,
   Michigan

Bobbie P. Hyder, Elementary Education Coordinator,
   Madison County School System, Huntsville,
   Alabama

Theodore Kaltsounis, Professor and Associate Dean,
   College of Education, University of Washington,
   Seattle, Washington

Richard H. Loftin, Former Director of Curriculum
   and Staff Development,
   Aldine Independent School District, Houston,
   Texas

Clyde P. Patton, Professor of Geography,
   University of Oregon, Eugene, Oregon

Norman J. G. Pounds, Former University Professor
   of Geography,
   Indiana University, Bloomington, Indiana

Arlene C. Rengert, Associate Professor of Geography,
   West Chester University, West Chester,
   Pennsylvania

Robert N. Saveland, Professor of Social Science
   Education,
   University of Georgia, Athens, Georgia

William J. Switala, Supervisor of Social Studies and
   Foreign Languages,
   Bethel Park School District, Bethel Park,
   Pennsylvania

Edgar A. Toppin, Professor of History and Dean of
   the Graduate School,
   Virginia State University, Petersburg, Virginia

GRADE-LEVEL CONTRIBUTORS

Wanda Allen, Teacher,
   Rankin Elementary School, Rankin, Pennsylvania

Harry Carnahan, Teacher,
   McKinley Elementary School, York, Pennsylvania

Anne Howlett, Teacher,
   Calypso School, Bethlehem, Pennsylvania

Edmund E. Jones, Teacher,
   Blue Ridge Elementary School, New Milford,
   Pennsylvania

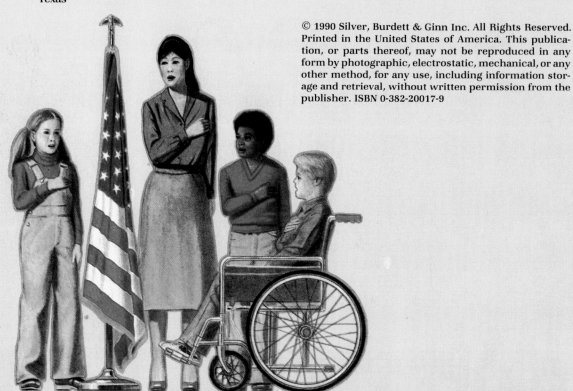

CONTENTS

MAPS

SPECIAL INTEREST MATERIALS

TIME LINES

DIAGRAMS AND GRAPHS

Dear Student,

Pennsylvania is a special place. It is a state that has mountains, hills, valleys, and plains. It also has hundreds of lakes, rivers and streams. You can swim, fish, hike, camp, and ski all over our state.

Pennsylvania is also a state with a long history. It was one of the first places settled by the Europeans in America. Over the years, Pennsylvania became the home of all kinds of people. The Declaration of Independence and the Constitution were both written in our state. Important battles in the Revolutionary and Civil Wars were fought here.

Pennsylvania is also a place of famous cities. People from all over the country and the world come here to visit our fine museums, art galleries, parks, zoos, and to see the many sports teams we have.

As you read this book you will learn about the history and geography of our home state. Learning all about Pennsylvania will be fun. When you finish this book, you will understand why Pennsylvania is such a special place to live.

Sincerely,
William J. Switala

Pennsylvania—Our Home

1 Pennsylvania's Land and Climate

Finding Pennsylvania on a Map

States and boundaries Do you remember the last time you looked at a map of the United States? When you did, you saw that it was divided into 50 parts. Each of these parts is called a **state.** Together the states make up one big country. That is why our country is called the United States of America.

You live in the state of Pennsylvania. You are about to learn more about Pennsylvania. You will learn about its people. You will find out where they live and how they make a living. You will also learn about the rich **history** of our state. History is the study of the past. In this chapter you will begin to learn about the **geography** of Pennsylvania. Geography is the study of the earth and how people use it.

The map on the next page shows the whole United States. As you can see, Pennsylvania is in the eastern part of our country. The lines around Pennsylvania separate it from other states. These lines are boundary lines. Another name for a boundary line is a border.

Look at the map again. Do you see the boundary line between Pennsylvania and Ohio, the state to its west? It is a straight line. It was made by people. It shows where one state ends and another begins. This type of boundary line is called a **political boundary.**

Now take a look at the eastern part of Pennsylvania. Do you see where it borders, or touches, New Jersey, the state to its east? This boundary line is crooked. If you were to go there, you would see that this boundary line is really the Delaware River. Sometimes a river, lake, or mountain range forms a boundary between two states. This is called a **natural boundary.** Pennsylvania's eastern political boundary follows the natural boundary line of a river. Look at the other boundary lines of Pennsylvania on the map. Do any of the other political boundaries run along natural boundary lines? What states besides Ohio and New Jersey border Pennsylvania?

The crooked course of the Delaware River is clear in this picture. On the left side of the river is Pennsylvania. On the right is New Jersey.

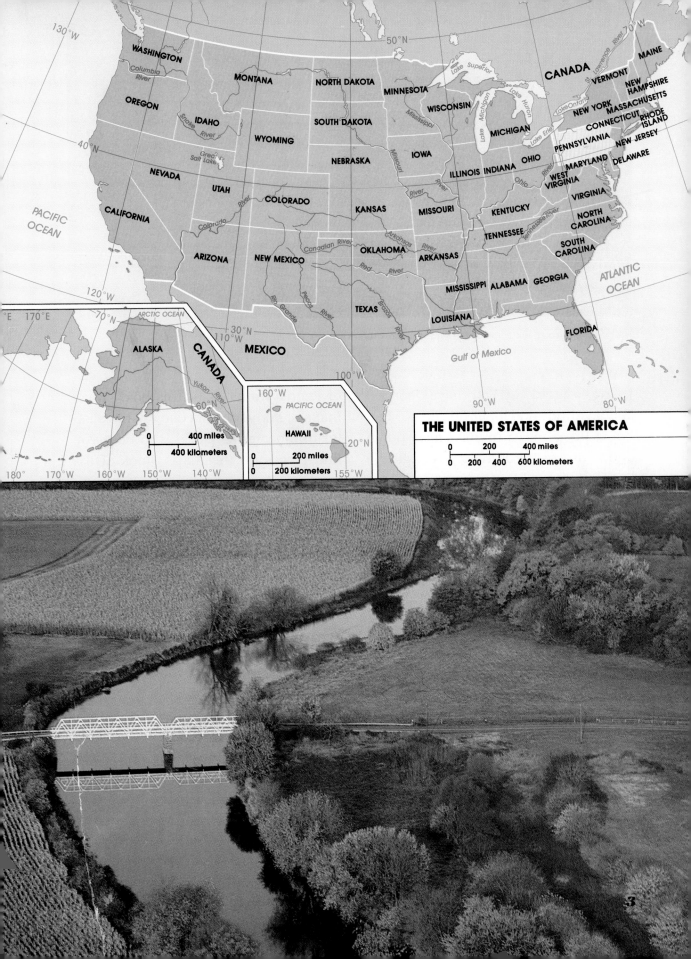

WASHINGTON
OREGON
MONTANA
NORTH DAKOTA
MINNESOTA
WISCONSIN
MICHIGAN
CANADA
VERMONT
MAINE
NEW HAMPSHIRE
NEW YORK
MASSACHUSETTS
CONNECTICUT
RHODE ISLAND
IDAHO
WYOMING
SOUTH DAKOTA
IOWA
PENNSYLVANIA
NEW JERSEY
NEVADA
UTAH
COLORADO
NEBRASKA
ILLINOIS INDIANA OHIO
MARYLAND
DELAWARE
WEST VIRGINIA
CALIFORNIA
KANSAS
MISSOURI
KENTUCKY
VIRGINIA
NORTH CAROLINA
PACIFIC OCEAN
ARIZONA
NEW MEXICO
OKLAHOMA
ARKANSAS
TENNESSEE
SOUTH CAROLINA
ATLANTIC OCEAN
TEXAS
MISSISSIPPI ALABAMA GEORGIA
LOUISIANA
FLORIDA
MEXICO
Gulf of Mexico

Columbia River
Snake River
Great Salt Lake
Colorado River
Rio Grande
Pecos River
Red River
Brazos River
Canadian River
Arkansas River
Missouri River
Mississippi
Ohio River
Tennessee River
Lake Superior
Lake Michigan
Lake Huron
Lake Erie
Lake Ontario
St. Lawrence River

130°W
120°W
50°N
40°N
30°N
100°W
90°W
80°W
70°W

ARCTIC OCEAN
ALASKA
CANADA
Yukon River
70°N
60°N
170°E
180°
170°W
160°W
150°W
140°W
110°W

0   400 miles
0   400 kilometers

HAWAII
PACIFIC OCEAN
160°W
20°N
155°W

0   200 miles
0   200 kilometers

THE UNITED STATES OF AMERICA

0   200   400 miles
0   200   400   600 kilometers

3

The city of Harrisburg is located on the Susquehanna River.

Using a grid　You have learned about latitude and longitude lines. Latitude lines measure distances north and south of the Equator. Longitude lines measure distances east and west of the Prime Meridian. As you can see on the map on page 5, latitude and longitude lines cross each other on maps. These crossing lines form a system of boxes called a **grid.** A grid can help you find places on a map.

Sometimes the grid boxes on a map have numbers and letters. Look at the map of Pennsylvania on the next page. Down the side of the map are the letters *A, B, C,* and *D.* Along the top of the map you can see the numbers 1, 2, 3, 4, 5, 6, and 7. Put a finger on the letter *C.* Now put a finger of your other hand on the number 5. Move both fingers, one down and one across, until they meet. This is box C-5. Harrisburg, the capital of Pennsylvania, is in this box. Road maps of Pennsylvania usually have letter-number grids like this to help you find places on the map. Look at the road map on page 170. Is your community shown? What box is it in?

Counties and cities　States can be divided into smaller parts called **counties.** These also have natural or political boundaries. There are 67 counties in Pennsylvania. You will read more about Pennsylvania's counties in Chapter 10.

There are about 50 cities in the counties of Pennsylvania. Cities are places where large numbers of people live and work. This is because many businesses and industries are found in cities. Do you live in or near a city? If so, which one?

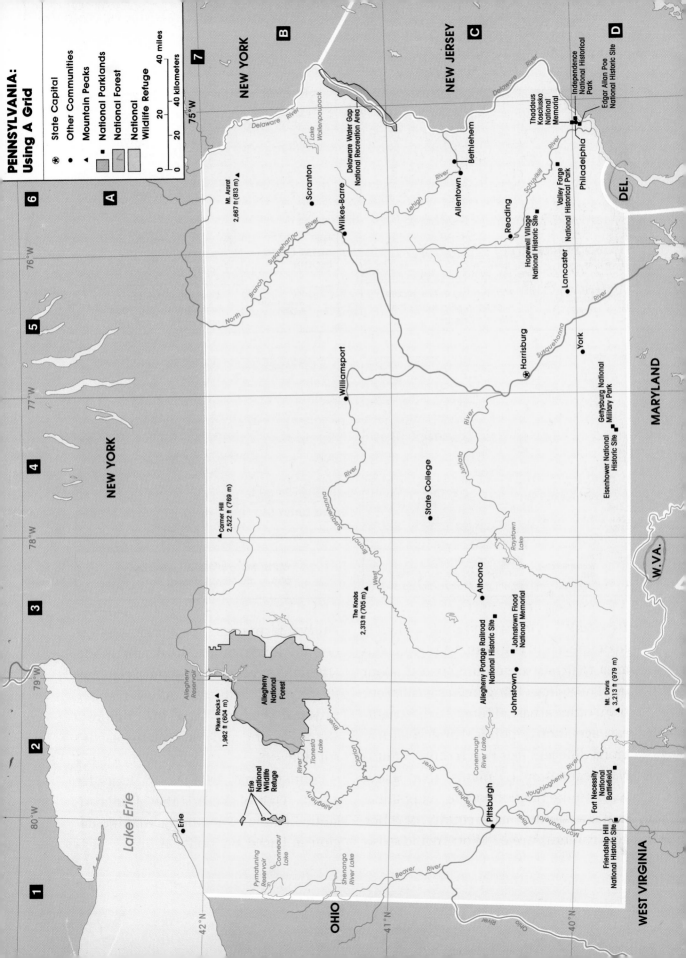

PENNSYLVANIA:
Using A Grid

- ⊛ State Capital
- • Other Communities
- ▲ Mountain Peaks
- ■ National Parklands
- National Forest
- National Wildlife Refuge

| 0 | 20 | 40 miles |
| 0 | 20 | 40 kilometers |

NEW YORK

NEW JERSEY

DEL.

MARYLAND

WEST VIRGINIA

OHIO

W. VA.

Lake Erie

Erie

Erie National Wildlife Refuge

Pymatuning Reservoir

Conneaut Lake

Shenango River Lake

Allegheny Reservoir

Pikes Rocks ▲
1,982 ft (604 m)

Allegheny National Forest

Tionesta Lake

Clarion River

Allegheny River

Beaver River

Ohio River

Pittsburgh

Fort Necessity National Battlefield

Friendship Hill National Historic Site

Mt. Davis ▲
3,213 ft (979 m)

Monongahela River

Youghiogheny River

Johnstown

Allegheny Portage Railroad National Historic Site

Johnstown Flood National Memorial

Conemaugh River Lake

Altoona

The Knobs ▲
2,313 ft (705 m)

Raystown Lake

State College

Juniata River

Susquehanna River

West Branch

Williamsport

Carmer Hill ▲
2,522 ft (769 m)

Mt. Ararat ▲
2,667 ft (813 m)

North Branch

Susquehanna River

Scranton

Wilkes-Barre

Delaware Water Gap National Recreation Area

Lake Wallenpaupack

Delaware River

Allentown

Bethlehem

Lehigh River

Harrisburg ⊛

York

Gettysburg National Military Park

Eisenhower National Historic Site

Lancaster

Hopewell Village National Historic Site

Reading

Schuylkill River

Valley Forge National Historical Park

Philadelphia

Thaddeus Kosciusko National Memorial

Independence National Historical Park

Edgar Allan Poe National Historic Site

Delaware River

80°W 79°W 78°W 77°W 76°W 75°W

42°N 41°N 40°N

1 2 3 4 5 6 7

A B C D

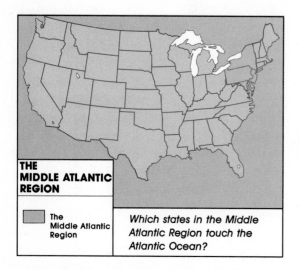

THE MIDDLE ATLANTIC REGION

The Middle Atlantic Region

Which states in the Middle Atlantic Region touch the Atlantic Ocean?

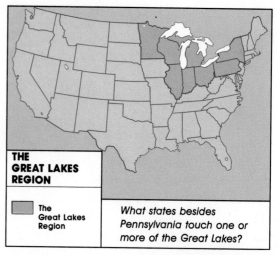

THE GREAT LAKES REGION

The Great Lakes Region

What states besides Pennsylvania touch one or more of the Great Lakes?

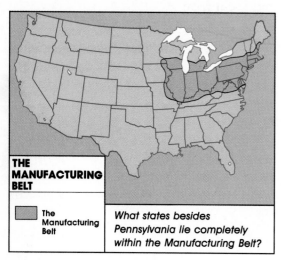

THE MANUFACTURING BELT

The Manufacturing Belt

What states besides Pennsylvania lie completely within the Manufacturing Belt?

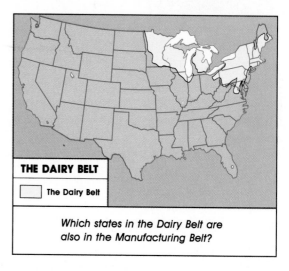

THE DAIRY BELT

The Dairy Belt

Which states in the Dairy Belt are also in the Manufacturing Belt?

Regions   One way to study a place is to divide it into **regions.** A region is an area that has something special about it. The special thing makes it different from other areas. Things such as natural vegetation or political units make regions different from each other. Natural vegetation is plants that grow without the help of people. A political unit is a country, state, county, or other government area. You could also study a farm region or a region where certain kinds of products are made. Often the special thing about a region is its physical features. As you know, physical features are the different shapes of land and water on the earth's surface.

Pennsylvania belongs to four regions. One of these is the Middle Atlantic Region. The Middle Atlantic Region is based on political units. It is

made up of the states that are between those in the Northeast and those in the South. Most of the Middle Atlantic states are near the Atlantic Ocean. Look at the map on page 6. Name the states in this region.

Pennsylvania touches Lake Erie at its northwestern border. Other states also touch one or more of the Great Lakes. States that do this belong to the Great Lakes Region. A physical feature, the Great Lakes, makes this region different from others.

The Manufacturing Belt is another kind of region. Manufacturing is the making of articles by hand or machine, especially in large quantities. This region has many factories where many different things are made. Steel, glass, cement, paper, and furniture are made in factories in Pennsylvania. Our state is an important member of the Manufacturing Belt.

Pennsylvania is part of four different regions. Two of the regions are the Manufacturing Belt and the Dairy Belt. In the photo above, cement is being made in a Pennsylvania factory. Below, is a dairy farm located in our state's Dairy Belt.

Pennsylvania is also a farming state. Farmers raise large herds of dairy cattle here. Milk, cheese, and other dairy products are produced in large amounts in our state. Because of this, Pennsylvania is part of the farm region called the Dairy Belt.

CHECKUP

1. What six states border, or touch, Pennsylvania?
2. How is a grid on a map formed?
3. To what regions does Pennsylvania belong?

7

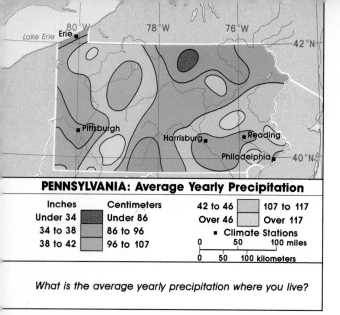

PENNSYLVANIA: Average Yearly Precipitation

Inches	Centimeters		
Under 34	Under 86	42 to 46	107 to 117
34 to 38	86 to 96	Over 46	Over 117
38 to 42	96 to 107	■ Climate Stations	

0   50   100 miles
0   50   100 kilometers

What is the average yearly precipitation where you live?

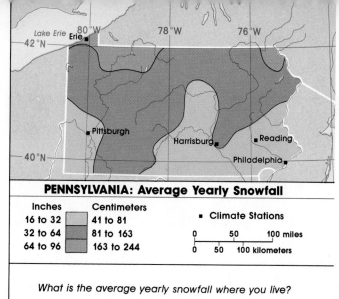

PENNSYLVANIA: Average Yearly Snowfall

Inches	Centimeters	
16 to 32	41 to 81	■ Climate Stations
32 to 64	81 to 163	
64 to 96	163 to 244	

0   50   100 miles
0   50   100 kilometers

What is the average yearly snowfall where you live?

Pennsylvania's Climate

> **VOCABULARY**
>
> weather   precipitation
> temperature   climate
> humidity

Weather Have you ever heard people talk about the **weather**? They probably used words such as *hot, cold, snowy, rainy, sunny,* and *windy.* Weather is the way the air is at a certain time in a given place.

Weather has many parts. One of these is air **temperature.** Temperature tells how hot or cold something is. A thermometer is used to measure temperature. In the summer the temperature of the air is usually high. The air is hot. In the winter the air temperature is usually lower than in the summer. The air is cold.

Humidity (hyü mid′ ə tē) is another part of weather. It tells how much moisture or water there is in the air. When the humidity is high, there is a lot of water in the air. High humidity can make you feel uncomfortable. When the humidity is high, people may say that the weather is muggy. When it is low, there is less water in the air and you usually feel more comfortable.

Precipitation You now know that weather is made up of temperature and humidity. On some days, weather also includes **precipitation** (pri sip ə tā′ shən). Precipitation is the moisture that falls to the earth. It can fall as rain, snow, sleet, or hail.

Look at the yearly precipitation map on this page. It shows that all parts of Pennsylvania receive some precipitation. Some precipitation falls each month. In the summer it falls as rain. In the winter most of the precipitation in Pennsylvania is snow. The yearly

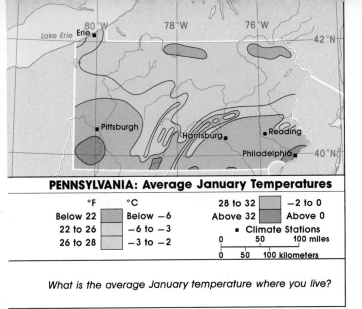

PENNSYLVANIA: Average January Temperatures

°F	°C		°F	°C
Below 22	Below −6		28 to 32	−2 to 0
22 to 26	−6 to −3		Above 32	Above 0
26 to 28	−3 to −2		■ Climate Stations	

0   50   100 miles
0   50   100 kilometers

What is the average January temperature where you live?

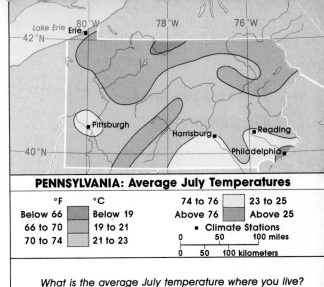

PENNSYLVANIA: Average July Temperatures

°F	°C		°F	°C
Below 66	Below 19		74 to 76	23 to 25
66 to 70	19 to 21		Above 76	Above 25
70 to 74	21 to 23		■ Climate Stations	

0   50   100 miles
0   50   100 kilometers

What is the average July temperature where you live?

snowfall map shows how much snow Pennsylvania gets.

Climate   We know that the weather changes every day. On some days it rains. On others it is sunny. Sometimes it is cold, and sometimes it is hot. People often ask what the weather is going to be like tomorrow.

There is another way to think about weather. You might ask what the weather in a place is like for a whole year. When you ask a question like this, you are really asking about the **climate** of a place. Climate is the weather a place has over a long time.

Pennsylvania gets plenty of precipitation. It also has a climate with a big difference in temperature between the coldest and hottest days in the year. Look at the maps Average January Temperatures and Average July Temperatures. What is the difference between the average January tempera-

tures and the average July temperatures in Philadelphia? Compare that to the difference between the average temperatures for the same 2 months in Erie.

Pennsylvania also has certain kinds of storms each year. One of these is the thunderstorm. Thunderstorms usually happen in the summer. Thunderstorms have lightning, thunder, strong winds, and a lot of rain. Sometimes tornadoes come from thunderstorms. Tornadoes are very strong, twisting winds. They do much damage. We also have blizzards in the winter. These are storms with very strong winds, cold temperatures, and a lot of snow.

CHECKUP
1. What is the difference between weather and climate?
2. Name four kinds of precipitation.
3. What kinds of storms do we have in Pennsylvania?

9

Pennsylvania's Natural Resources

Natural resources   Some places have lots of water, but others do not. One part of the country has good soil for farming, but another has little or none. Some areas are covered by forests, but others have few or no trees.

Some states have large amounts of **minerals,** but others do not. Minerals are things found in the earth that are neither plant nor animal. *Water, soil, forests,* and *minerals* are all **natural resources.** Natural resources are things made by nature that are useful to people. Pennsylvania is lucky because it has many natural resources. Let us take a look at the most important of Pennsylvania's natural resources.

Rivers   Pennsylvania has three large **river systems.** A river system is a group of streams and smaller rivers that flow into a big river. These streams and rivers drain water from a

Rafting is popular on the Youghiogheny River, which is part of the Ohio River system.

Hydroelectric power plants make electricity by using the power of falling water. Pennsylvania has a number of hydroelectric power plants.

large area of land. The three big river systems in Pennsylvania are the Delaware in the east, the Susquehanna (səs kwə han′ ə) in the center of the state, and the Ohio in the west. Look at the map on page 171 to see the areas these rivers drain.

Rivers have many uses. They are a source of pure drinking water. They can also be used as highways. Goods can be moved on a river on long, flat boats without motors. These boats are called barges. Barges are pushed by other boats. They are a cheap way to move goods on a river.

Hydroelectric power can be made on a river. Hydroelectric power is electricity made by the power of falling water. Dams are built on rivers to make the water fall. When water falls from behind a dam, it turns wheels at a power station. The turning wheels drive machines that make electric power. The electricity is sent through power lines for use in homes, factories, and other buildings.

People also use rivers for recreation. Some people like to fish in rivers. Others enjoy boating, swimming, and waterskiing on rivers in our state.

Soil   Most of the soil in Pennsylvania is good for some type of farming. But the soil in some parts of the state is better than in others. The soil in the southeastern part of our state and around Lake Erie is especially good for farming. It contains many minerals that plants need. One of these minerals is limestone. The soil in these two parts of Pennsylvania has large amounts of limestone. Many kinds of vegetables, grains, and fruit trees are grown here. Grains are cereal plants such as corn, wheat, and oats. They are important foods for both people

This mushroom farmer wears a cap with a lamp to pick mushrooms. Mushrooms are grown in the dark.

On this farm in southeastern Pennsylvania, the grain crop is harvested and set in neat stacks.

and animals. The soil in the center and the northern part of our state is good for growing grains. Because of this the farmers in these areas find it easy to raise dairy cattle.

Pennsylvania has about 60,000 farms. Corn, oats, wheat, hay, and potatoes are important crops in Pennsylvania. Large amounts of apples, peaches, and grapes are grown in the state. Pennsylvania is also the largest producer of mushrooms in the country. Farmers in Pennsylvania also raise hogs, beef and dairy cattle, sheep, chickens, and turkeys.

Forests If you take a trip across our state, you will see millions of trees. More than half of Pennsylvania is covered by forests. Trees grow especially well in the northern region of our state. When people first came here, they found great forests of oak, maple, pine, and hemlock. Many of these trees were cut down for their wood. The wood was used for building. It was also used for heating and cooking. Until the 1880s, Pennsylvania led the other states in our country in forest products. Wood from Pennsylvania was used to make ships, houses, furniture, barrels, charcoal, and railroad ties, rails and cars.

Today the forests are still important to Pennsylvania. The great oak and maple forests are gone, but there are still many pine and hemlock trees. The wood is now used to make paper and furniture. Pennsylvania is also a leading producer of Christmas trees. Indiana County in western Pennsylvania, where many Christmas trees are grown, calls itself the Christmas Tree Capital of the World.

These logs are being loaded for shipment. They may be used later to make paper.

Minerals   Millions of years ago Pennsylvania was a wet and swampy place. When the shape of the land changed, many trees, plants, and animals were covered by layers of rock. Slowly the remains of the trees, plants, and animals changed. They became pockets of minerals such as coal, oil, and natural gas. Coal, oil, and natural gas are minerals that can be used as **fuels.** A fuel is something that can be burned to make heat or power.

Two kinds of coal are found in Pennsylvania. One kind is **bituminous** (bə tü′ mə nəs), or soft, coal. It is very plentiful in western and central Pennsylvania. It burns easily but gives off a lot of smoke. It is used in making steel. Because a lot of bituminous coal

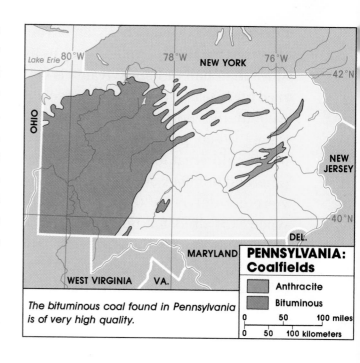

The bituminous coal found in Pennsylvania is of very high quality.

PENNSYLVANIA: Coalfields

- Anthracite
- Bituminous

0   50   100 miles
0   50   100 kilometers

Long ago, plants and trees such as these fell into the swamps in Pennsylvania. Rock covered the plants. Minerals formed in the layers between the rock as the rock and plant layers were pressed and folded.

is found around Pittsburgh, that city became a center for making steel. The other kind of coal found in Pennsylvania is **anthracite** (an′ thrə sīt), or hard coal. It is found mainly in eastern Pennsylvania around Scranton and Hazleton. It burns more slowly than bituminous coal and lasts longer. It gives off far less smoke. Because of this, anthracite is a better coal for heating homes and other buildings. Coal mining is an important industry in Pennsylvania. It gives many people jobs and brings a large amount of money to the state.

Coal is mined in two ways. One of these is called surface, or strip, mining. Surface mining is the way that most of the anthracite and bituminous coal in Pennsylvania is mined. This type of mining is used when the coal is near the surface. Large bulldozers are used to strip away the soil and rock that lie on top of the coal. Then great power shovels and other machines are used to remove the coal. The coal is put into trucks and carried away. After all the coal has been removed, the soil is put back over the ground where the coal was mined. Grass and trees are planted so that the land looks beautiful again.

A power shovel removes coal at a strip mine in Schuylkill County.

New grass and trees make land once used for strip mining a perfect place for a Boy Scout Jamboree.

Another way to mine coal is underground mining. Some of the anthracite and bituminous coal in our state is mined in underground mines. In underground mining, two shafts, or large holes, are dug into the ground. The shafts are dug straight down if the coal is very deep in the earth. This type of underground mine is a shaft mine. It is used mostly for bituminous coal, which can lie 400 to 600 feet (122 to 183 m) down in the ground. Anthracite usually lies at an angle and is not found as deep, so the shafts are dug on a slant. This type of mine is a slope mine. In both types of underground mines, the miners go in and out through one shaft. Tunnels are dug off

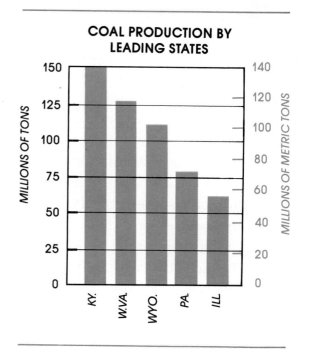

COAL PRODUCTION BY LEADING STATES

Pennsylvania is the fourth leading state in the United States in the production of coal.

One way that coal is mined in Pennsylvania is through shaft mines.

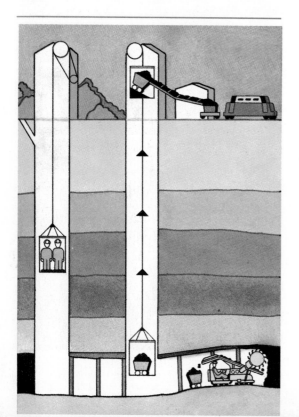

the shafts into the coal. Large machines are used to drill and scoop out the coal. It is then hauled to the surface through the second shaft.

Another important Pennsylvania mineral is oil. The first oil well in the world was drilled in Titusville, Pennsylvania, in 1859. For many years after that, Pennsylvania was the leader in producing oil. Today, oil earns around $100 million a year for the state. Pennsylvania oil is especially good when used as a **lubricant** (lü′ bri kənt). A lubricant is something that helps machines run smoothly.

A third important mineral resource found in Pennsylvania is natural gas.

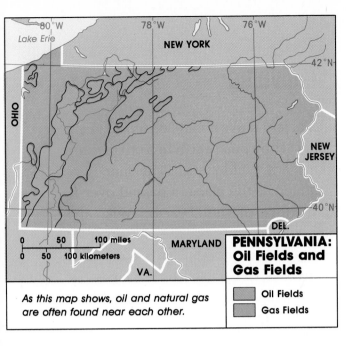

As this map shows, oil and natural gas are often found near each other.

PENNSYLVANIA: Oil Fields and Gas Fields

☐ Oil Fields
☐ Gas Fields

Natural gas is a clear, odorless gas used as a source of heat. In many areas it has taken the place of coal as a way to heat homes and factories. It gives off no smoke and leaves no ashes. Natural gas is found in many places in western Pennsylvania.

CHECKUP

1. Name four of Pennsylvania's natural resources.
2. What farm crops grow well in Pennsylvania?
3. How were coal, oil, and natural gas formed?

1/CHAPTER REVIEW

Some Key Terms On a piece of paper write the words missing from the sentences below. Use these words: *natural resources, region, bituminous, fuel,* and *political boundary.*

1. A line that forms the border between places on a map is called a _____ .
2. A _____ is something that can be burned to make heat or power.
3. A _____ is an area that has something special about it that makes it different from other areas.
4. _____ are things made by nature that are useful to people.
5. Soft, or _____ , coal burns easily and gives off a lot of smoke.

Do Some Research Use an encyclopedia or other reference book to find the answers to the following questions.

1. Do any of the political boundaries of the United States run along natural boundaries?
2. Through what states besides Pennsylvania does the Ohio River flow?
3. Where is coal mined in the United States today?

For Thought Write a paragraph or two in answer to one of the following questions.

1. How does being part of the Manufacturing Belt affect Pennsylvania?
2. How can the people of Pennsylvania take care of the state's forests?

2 The Five Regions of Pennsylvania

How Pennsylvania Was Formed

```
┌─ VOCABULARY ─────────────────┐
│  glacier        ridge         │
│  drift          moraine       │
└───────────────────────────────┘
```

Glaciers change the land   The shape of the land in North America has changed over millions of years. Because of the changes that took place, five physical regions developed in Pennsylvania. They are the Atlantic Coastal Plain, the Erie Plain, the Piedmont (pēd′ mänt), the Ridge and Valley Region, and the Allegheny Plateau (al ə gā′ nē pla tō′).

About a million years ago, the earth got cooler. The winters were longer. A large amount of snow fell. Because the temperature stayed cold, the snow did not melt. It got deeper and deeper. Slowly the snow grew into thick sheets of ice. These sheets are called **glaciers** (glā′ sherz). Some were over 2 miles (3 km) thick. Because of their great weight, the glaciers began to push south from the area around the North Pole. Some came as far south as Pennsylvania.

Glaciers move about 300 feet (91 m) a year. They push earth in front of them like giant bulldozers. The land was changed as the glaciers passed over it. A mixture of sand, earth, rock, and stones was carried by the glaciers from one place to another. This mixture is known as **drift.** In some places the drift formed long strips of raised land called **ridges.** A ridge made by drift is called a **moraine** (mə rān′). But only some of the ridges on the land were formed by drift. Some ridges were pushed up out of the earth. Valleys formed between the ridges. Some of the ridges were worn down by rain and wind.

The glaciers moved across northern Pennsylvania. They moved as far south as Northampton, Schuylkill (skül′ kil), and Northumberland counties in the east and Beaver and Butler counties in the west. The land in Moraine State Park in Butler County was formed by a glacier. As the summers got warmer, the glaciers began to melt. They left behind great amounts of water. In western Pennsylvania the Allegheny River was formed by a glacier. In the center of Pennsylvania,

The map shows Pennsylvania's five regions. Great ice sheets like the Alaskan glacier shown at right once covered northern Pennsylvania, and changed the shape of the land.

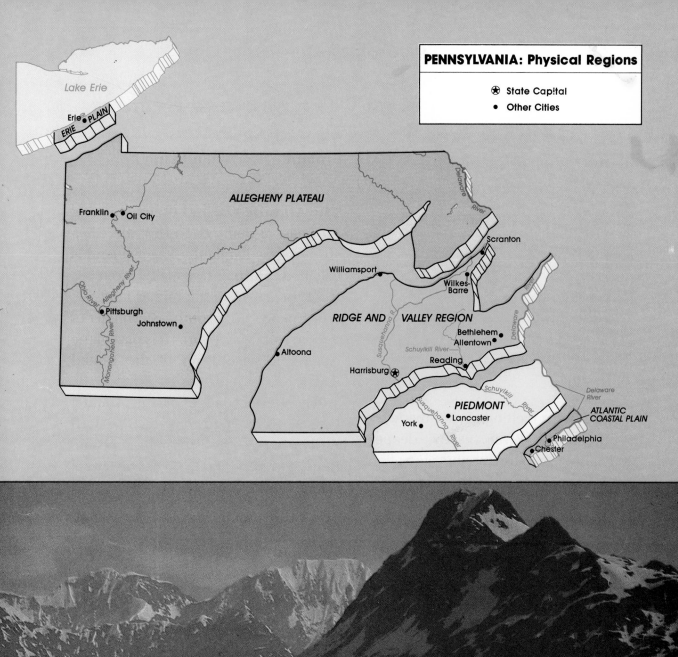

Lake Erie

Erie ERIE PLAIN

ALLEGHENY PLATEAU

Franklin • Oil City

Delaware River

Scranton

Williamsport

Wilkes-Barre

Ohio River Allegheny River

Pittsburgh

Johnstown

RIDGE AND VALLEY REGION

Bethlehem

Allentown

Susquehanna R.

Schuylkill River

Delaware

Monongahela River

Altoona

Reading

Harrisburg ⊛

Schuylkill River

PIEDMONT

Delaware River

York

Lancaster

Susquehanna River

ATLANTIC COASTAL PLAIN

Philadelphia

Chester

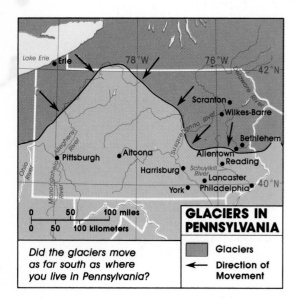

GLACIERS IN PENNSYLVANIA

Did the glaciers move as far south as where you live in Pennsylvania?

Glaciers

← Direction of Movement

water from a melting glacier made the Susquehanna River valley deeper. Rain also made streams and rivers flow with water.

All of these changes helped make the five physical regions of Pennsylvania. It would be very hard to study all of the state at once. To make it easier, we can think of Pennsylvania as a giant jigsaw puzzle. Each piece of the puzzle is a region of the state. When we put all of the pieces together, we have a picture that says, "This is Pennsylvania!" Now let's look at the pieces of the Pennsylvania puzzle.

CHECKUP

1. What are the five physical regions of Pennsylvania?
2. What is a glacier?
3. How is a moraine formed?

The Lowland Regions

┌─ VOCABULARY ─────────────────┐
plain   **Fall Line**
└──────────────────────────────┘

The Atlantic Coastal Plain   Along the coast of many countries, there is a strip of low, flat land. This flat land is called a **plain.** It usually stretches from the ocean to the higher land farther inland. The southeastern part of Pennsylvania is a plain. It is part of the Atlantic Coastal Plain of the United States.

The western edge of the Atlantic Coastal Plain is formed by the **Fall Line.** On the other side of the Fall Line is the Piedmont region. The Fall Line is a line of small waterfalls and rapids. Rapids are places in rivers or streams where the water flows very quickly and roughly. The Fall Line is formed by streams flowing from the older, harder rocks on the west to the softer rocks on the east. The flowing streams erode, or wash away, the softer rocks of the coastal plain. This causes the rivers and streams to fall, or drop, 40 to 70 feet (12 to 21 m) at the Fall Line.

Many towns and cities grew up along the Fall Line because people and goods could be moved easily up the rivers and streams to that point from the Atlantic Ocean. Philadelphia was founded on the Fall Line near the rapids in the Schuylkill River.

Because the Atlantic Ocean and the Delaware River are nearby, materials from all over the world are brought to the Atlantic Coastal Plain in Pennsylvania. Factories in the region use many of these materials. Ships are built here. Large plants where oil is changed into gasoline and other products line the Delaware River near Philadelphia and Chester. Millions of people live and work in this region of Pennsylvania. Philadelphia, the largest city in our state, is one of only six cities in the United States that have populations of more than 1 million.

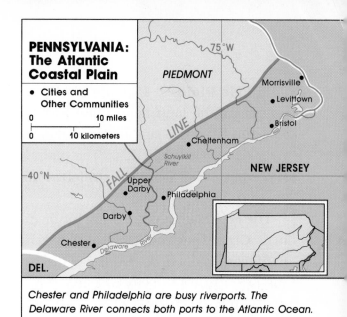

PENNSYLVANIA: The Atlantic Coastal Plain

• Cities and Other Communities

Chester and Philadelphia are busy riverports. The Delaware River connects both ports to the Atlantic Ocean.

Is your community on the Atlantic Coastal Plain? That region has a great many industries that are related to shipping. Here an oil tanker leaves a Chester shipyard.

The Erie Plain Like the land near an ocean, the land near a lake can be low and flat. The land in Pennsylvania near Lake Erie is like this. The plain is not very wide, but it stretches all around the lake.

The Erie Plain has good soil for farming. Grapevines and large orchards of fruit trees grow here. At the center of the Erie Plain is the city of Erie. It has many manufacturing plants. Paper, cloth, and tools are made here. Erie is also an important recreation area. People from all over Pennsylvania come to the Erie area to fish, sail, and swim. Presque Isle State Park is a favorite vacation spot on Lake Erie. Have you and your family ever spent a vacation in this part of Pennsylvania?

This vineyard lies close to Lake Erie, which may be seen in the distance. Fruit and vegetables grow well in the fertile soil of the Erie Plain.

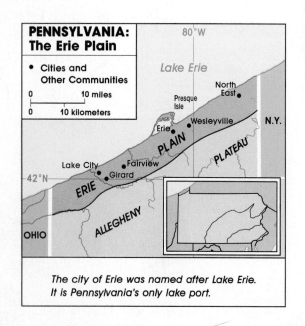

The city of Erie was named after Lake Erie. It is Pennsylvania's only lake port.

CHECKUP

1. What is a plain?
2. What is the largest city in Pennsylvania?
3. In which lowland region is the soil especially good for growing grapes and other fruit?

The Upland Regions

The Piedmont   The word **piedmont** means "the land at the foot of the mountains." The land is higher than a plain, but not as high as a mountain. The Piedmont Region of the United States separates the coastal plain from the mountains. It stretches from New York to Alabama. In Pennsylvania the Piedmont starts east of Philadelphia. It stretches west towards Harrisburg, our state capital, and north towards the Blue Mountains. The Piedmont is a place of low hills and wide valleys.

The Schuylkill and Susquehanna rivers flow through the Piedmont. There are many factories along the Schuylkill. Steel, machinery, and paper are made in this area. The Piedmont has especially good soil. Some of the best farmland in the United States is found in Pennsylvania's Piedmont Region. Crops of all kinds grow well in the region. Some of these important crops are corn, wheat, and alfalfa. At the center of the Piedmont is the city of Lancaster. Hundreds of fine farms can be seen around the city. In the western part of the Piedmont is the city of York. It is a manufacturing center. And like Lancaster, York is surrounded by excellent farmland.

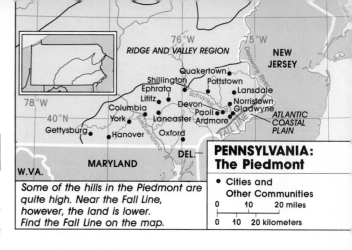

Some of the hills in the Piedmont are quite high. Near the Fall Line, however, the land is lower. Find the Fall Line on the map.

PENNSYLVANIA: The Piedmont

• Cities and Other Communities

0   10   20 miles

0   10   20 kilometers

Many good farms are found in the Piedmont Region. The farm shown in the picture below is in New Holland.

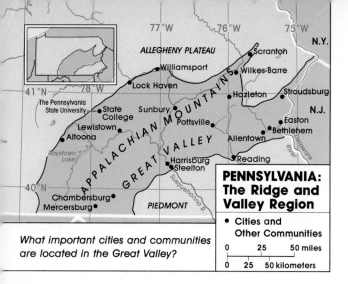

PENNSYLVANIA:
The Ridge and
Valley Region

• Cities and
Other Communities

0   25   50 miles

0   25   50 kilometers

*What important cities and communities
are located in the Great Valley?*

The Ridge and Valley Region   As
you travel north and west from the
Piedmont, you come to a chain of
mountain ridges and valleys. This is
the Ridge and Valley Region of Pennsylvania. It is part of a larger physical region that stretches from Maine to Alabama. The mountains in this region
are the Appalachian (ap ə lā′ chən)
Mountains. Between the rows of
mountain ridges are many deep valleys. Along the border between the
Ridge and Valley Region and the Piedmont, there is a very wide valley called
the Great Valley. It runs from Pennsylvania to Tennessee. The cities of Allentown and Bethlehem and many good
farms are found in the Great Valley.

The cities of Scranton and Wilkes-
Barre are in the Ridge and Valley Region. They are in the heart of the
anthracite coal-mining area. On the
northern edge of the region is the city
of Williamsport. For years, Williams-

*In the Ridge and Valley Region, rolling hills and wide valleys
stretch to the Allegheny Mountains.*

port was the center of the lumber industry in Pennsylvania. Lumber is
boards cut from logs. You may know
that Little League baseball began in Williamsport about 50 years ago. Towards
the southern edge of the Ridge and Valley Region are Reading and Harrisburg,
our state capital. The Pennsylvania
State University and the manufacturing
city of Altoona are along the western
edge of the Ridge and Valley Region.
Raystown Lake in the southwestern
part of the region has become a popular
place for fishing and boating.

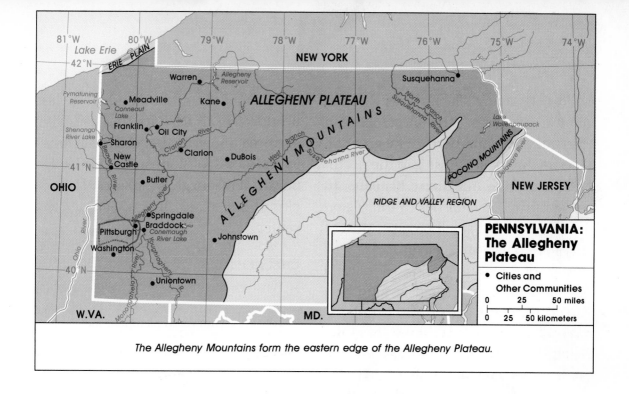

The Allegheny Mountains form the eastern edge of the Allegheny Plateau.

The Allegheny Plateau   A **plateau** is an area of land that is flat like a plain but is much higher. Most of western and northern Pennsylvania is a plateau. This region is called the Allegheny Plateau. It is part of a larger region of high, almost flat land that runs from Pennsylvania to the northeastern edge of Alabama. Thousands of years ago this land was flat. As the years passed, rain and the water from melting glaciers formed streams and rivers in the region. Slowly the streams and rivers wore paths through the plateau. Today the land is filled with streams and rivers. The plateau land now also has small, rounded hills and shallow valleys. At its eastern edge are the Allegheny Mountains. The northeastern part of the region includes the Pocono Mountains.

The Allegheny River forms the western boundary of the Allegheny National Forest.

25

The Allegheny Plateau is very rich in natural resources. The finest forests in the state are found here. The great Allegheny National Forest is in the northern part of the Allegheny Plateau. In the southwestern corner of the region are hundreds of small farms. Most of these are dairy-cattle farms.

Most of the bituminous coal, natural gas, and oil in our state is found on the Allegheny Plateau. Washington, Greene, Allegheny, Westmoreland, Indiana, and Cambria counties are the center of the bituminous coal industry. Much of the oil in the region is taken from the ground and made into products near Oil City and Franklin. All three minerals are used by factories in the cities of Johnstown and Pittsburgh. Pittsburgh is the second largest city in our state. It is a leading steel center.

CHECKUP

1. What are the three upland regions of Pennsylvania?
2. What does the word *piedmont* mean?
3. What two Pennsylvania cities are found in the Great Valley?
4. In which region is the center of the bituminous coal industry?

2 / CHAPTER REVIEW

Some Key Terms On a piece of paper, write in the words missing from the sentences below. Use these words: *glaciers, drift, plain, piedmont, moraine.*

1. The word _____ means "the land at the foot of the mountains."

2. A _____ is low, flat land.

3. Thick sheets of ice are called _____.

4. The mixture of sand, earth, rock, and stones that is carried by glaciers from one place to another is known as _____.

5. A _____ is a ridge formed by drift.

Do Some Research Use an encyclopedia or other reference book to find the answers to the following questions.

1. Where in the United States can you find glaciers today?

2. What large cities in other states are located on the Atlantic Coastal Plain?

3. What mountains in the United States are included in the Appalachian Mountain range?

For Thought Write a paragraph or two in answer to one of the following questions.

1. For what geographic reasons are Pennsylvania's two largest cities located where they are?

2. Why, do you think, are there factories along many of the rivers in Pennsylvania?

KEY FACTS

1. Political boundaries may also be natural boundaries.

2. Pennsylvania belongs to four regions: the Middle Atlantic Region, the Great Lakes Region, the Manufacturing Belt, and the Dairy Belt.

3. Temperature, precipitation, and humidity are important parts of weather.

4. Rivers, soil, forests, and minerals are the most important natural resources in Pennsylvania.

5. Pennsylvania's physical features were formed over a long period of time.

6. Pennsylvania has five physical regions: the Atlantic Coastal Plain, the Erie Plain, the Piedmont, the Ridge and Valley Region, and the Allegheny Plateau.

VOCABULARY QUIZ

Write the numbers 1 through 10 on a piece of paper. Match each term with its definition.

a. grid	f. river system
b. region	g. lubricant
c. glacier	h. hydroelectric power
d. humidity	i. anthracite
e. plateau	j. drift

1. A mixture of sand, earth, rock, and stones carried by glaciers

2. An area that has something special about it

3. Electricity made by the power of falling water

4. A system of crossing lines that form boxes on a map

5. A kind of coal that burns slowly with little smoke

6. A thick sheet of ice

7. The amount of moisture or water in the air

8. A high, almost flat area of land

9. A group of streams and rivers that drain water from a large area of land

10. Something that helps machines run smoothly

REVIEW QUESTIONS

1. What is a natural boundary?

2. How are weather and climate different?

3. Why is Pennsylvania in the Dairy Belt?

4. Why are rivers an important natural resource?

5. How do the five physical regions in Pennsylvania differ from one another?

ACTIVITIES

1. List at least five things in your home or in school that come from natural resources. Next to each item write at least one natural resource used to make it.

2. On an outline map of Pennsylvania, draw in and label the five physical regions. Then draw in the three main river systems. Use the maps on pages 19 and 171 to help you.

WHAT IS A MAP GRID?

You have learned that some maps have a grid, or system of lines that form boxes as they cross one another. The boxes are numbered across the top of the map. They are also lettered down the side of the map. You can use the letters and numbers to find places on a map.

SKILLS PRACTICE

Use the map grid below. Name the city or town that is located within each of the boxes formed by the following letters and numbers.

1. A-2
2. D-1
3. B-4

4. B-6
5. C-4

For examples 6 through 10, decide which letter-number location matches the activity you could do there.

6. Camping
7. Mountain climbing
8. Watching airplanes take off and land
9. Watching coal being mined
10. Watching cows being milked

a. D-2
b. A-6
c. A-1
d. C-3
e. A-3

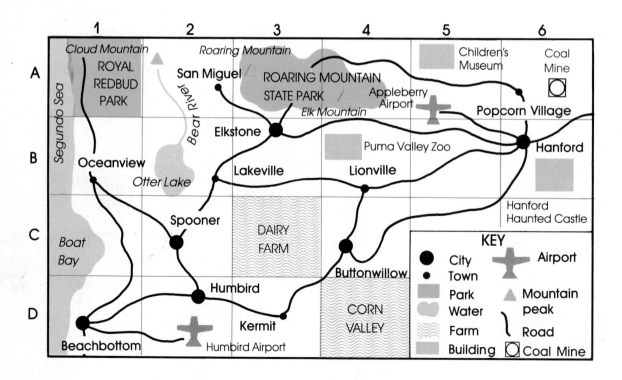

The Early Years in Pennsylvania

The Indians of Pennsylvania

> **VOCABULARY**
>
> | | |
> |---|---|
> | prehistory | tribe |
> | maize | Lenni-Lenape |
> | Woodland Indian | league |

The Indians come to America When Columbus came to America in 1492, he found people living here. Columbus called these people Indians because he thought he was in the land of India. Another name for the Indians is Native Americans. A native is a person who was born in a certain place or country or someone already living in a place or country when settlers from other countries arrive. The Indians had been living in America a long time when Columbus arrived.

No one knows for sure when the first Indians came to North America. Some scientists think that it was over 20,000 years ago. The Indians came from Asia, looking for good hunting grounds. At that time a strip of land about 50 miles (80 km) long joined Asia to North America. The Indians walked across this strip of land. Some of them stayed in North America. Others traveled as far south as South America.

These early Indians were hunters. They followed animals in the hunt. They did not stay anywhere for very long. The Indians used spears to hunt. They ate animal meat and used animal skins for clothing. Later they also ate fish and gathered wild plants to eat.

One way to learn about a people is to read the things they wrote. These writings are a people's history. The story of a people before they learned to write things down is their **prehistory.** The Indians did not leave any writings, so we can only learn about their prehistory. We can do this by studying the things the Indians left behind. We might study their spears, tools, pots, and the bones of the animals they ate.

We can learn about how Indians lived by studying the things they left behind. Look at the Indian objects on the opposite page. Can you tell what these objects are or what they were used for?

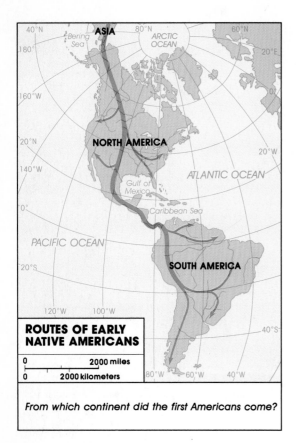

ROUTES OF EARLY NATIVE AMERICANS

0   2000 miles

0   2000 kilometers

From which continent did the first Americans come?

The earliest Indians in Pennsylvania More than 10,000 years ago, the Indians reached Pennsylvania. These were the Paleo (pā′ lē ō), or Old, Indians. They hunted, fished, and gathered food. About 3,000 years ago they learned to plant corn. They called it **maize** (māz). This was a big step. The corn gave them a good supply of food. Now they did not have to hunt as much. This new food made it possible for them to stay in one place. Because they made their homes in or near the woods, the Indians of Pennsylvania are called **Woodland Indians.**

The Indians began to build villages near their cornfields. They began to live together in groups called **tribes.** A tribe is a group held together by family, geography, or customs. The tribes picked leaders and made laws.

The Algonquians When people from Europe first came to northeastern America, they found two large groups of Indians. One group spoke a language called Algonquian (al gong′ kē ən). The main tribes in this group were the Delawares, the Nanticokes (nan tə′ kōks), and the Shawnees (shô′ nēz). The Delawares lived along the Delaware River. The Nanticokes made their homes near the North Branch of the Susquehanna River. The Shawnees lived to the west and along the lower part of the Susquehanna River. Find these Algonquian tribes on the map on page 33.

The Delawares were the most important Algonquian-speaking tribe in the area. They called themselves the **Lenni-Lenape** (le′ nē len′ ə pē), or Original People. The Europeans called them the Delaware Indians because they lived along the Delaware River. It was the Delawares who helped the Europeans live through their first winters in this part of the New World.

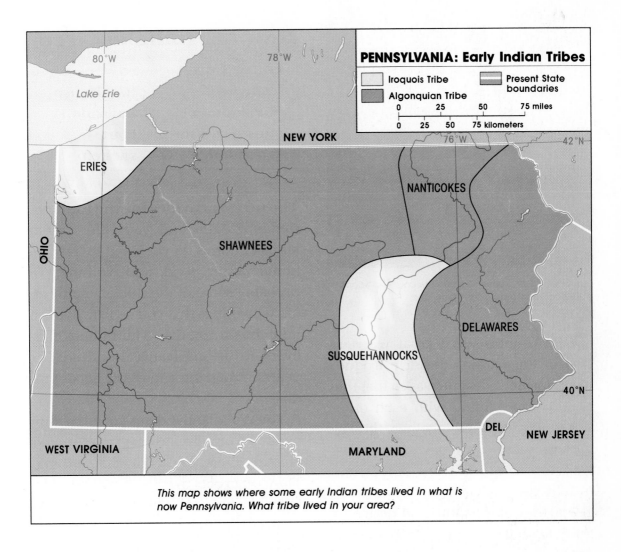

PENNSYLVANIA: Early Indian Tribes

Iroquois Tribe
Algonquian Tribe
Present State boundaries

0 25 50 75 miles
0 25 50 75 kilometers

80°W
Lake Erie
78°W
NEW YORK
76°W
42°N
ERIES
NANTICOKES
OHIO
SHAWNEES
DELAWARES
SUSQUEHANNOCKS
40°N
DEL.
NEW JERSEY
WEST VIRGINIA
MARYLAND

This map shows where some early Indian tribes lived in what is now Pennsylvania. What tribe lived in your area?

The Iroquois The other large group of Indians spoke the Iroquois (ir′ ə kwoi) language. About 500 years ago, five large Iroquois tribes formed a **league.** A league is a group of people that joins together for a common purpose. The five tribes were the Mohawks (mō′ hôks), Oneidas (ō nī′ dəz), Onondagas (on ən dô′ gəz), Cayugas (kā yü′ gəz), and Senecas (sen′ i kəz). Their league was known as the League of the Five Nations. These five tribes lived north of Pennsylvania. Two other Iroquoian-speaking tribes lived in Pennsylvania. One was the Eries, who lived on the southern shores of Lake Erie. The other was the Susquehannocks (səs kwə han′ əks), who lived along the Susquehanna River. Find the Iroquois tribes on the map on this page.

Uthawah was an Iroquois chief. The chiefs, or sachems, were chosen by the women of the tribe.

The Iroquois were great warriors. One of the reasons that five Iroquois tribes formed a league was so that they would stop fighting with each other. When they worked together, the Five Nations were very powerful. They went to war against many other tribes. In 1654, they defeated the Eries. In the 1670s, they came south and destroyed the Susquehannocks. The Tuscaroras (təs kə rôr′ əz) joined the five tribes after this, forming the League of the Six Nations. By 1776, the power of the Six Nations had spread all over Pennsylvania.

CHECKUP

1. What is prehistory?
2. What great discovery made it possible for the Indians to stay in one place and build villages?
3. Who were the Lenni-Lenape?

How the Indians Lived

```
┌─ VOCABULARY ──────────────────────┐
│   basic need          longhouse   │
│   environment         palisade    │
│   conservationist     clan        │
│   sweat lodge         sachem      │
└───────────────────────────────────┘
```

The forest provides for the Indians' needs   Think of your life. What kinds of things do you need to live? A home, water, food, and clothing are probably some of the things you think of. The things that you need to live are your **basic needs.** The Indians that lived in Pennsylvania hundreds of years ago had the same basic needs you do.

The Woodland Indians got what they needed from the forest. They hunted animals there for food and clothing. They dug roots there and picked nuts, fruit, and berries. They used trees and plants to build their homes. In the forest rivers and streams, they caught fish and turtles. The rivers and streams also gave them fresh water for drinking and bathing.

The Indians lived at peace with their **environment** (in vī′ rən mənt). The environment is all the things around us, such as water, land, animals, plants, and air. The Indians did not waste any of these things. They took only what they needed. A person who saves the environment and does not waste its gifts is called a **conservationist** (kän sər vā′ shə nəst). A conservationist uses the environment wisely. The Indians were good conservationists.

The Indians also met their needs by living in villages. There was food in the village. No one went hungry as long as there was food to share. The village also gave the Indians shelter and protection.

Algonquian villages Algonquian villages were made up of groups of small houses. Each house was made of a frame of branches and young trees. Sheets of bark or reed mats were used to cover the frame. The house had one opening, in the front. There was also a hole in the roof of the house. This hole let out the smoke from the fire. One family lived in each house.

The Algonquian villages also had a special house called a **sweat lodge.** Inside this small house the Algonquians took steam baths. Hot stones and rocks were brought into the lodge. Water was poured slowly over them. This made a lot of steam. The steam made those sitting in the lodge sweat. After sitting in the lodge, the Indians would run out and jump into some cold water, such as a river or stream. This was one way in which they kept clean.

Iroquois villages The Iroquois villages were not like those of the Algonquians. They were made up of large houses, not groups of small houses.

In an Indian village, one woman (left center) grinds corn in the hollowed top of a log. Another woman (left) prepares to skin a deer. Still another (right) weaves a mat.

These houses were usually around 60 feet (18 m) long. Some were even as long as 100 feet (30 m) or more. Because they were so long, these houses were called **longhouses.** The longhouses were made in much the same way as the Algonquians' small houses. But each longhouse had two openings, one at each end, and several openings in the roof. Many families lived in each longhouse.

The Iroquois also built fences of pointed logs around their villages. These were known as **palisades** (pal ə sādz'). They protected the villages from enemies and wild animals.

The Iroquois lived in longhouses. The Indians used young trees, called saplings, to form the longhouse's frame. Then they covered the frame with tree bark. Why do you think there were openings in the roof of the longhouse?

Corn, beans, and squash   Corn was the most important food the Indians had.   They did not plant it in rows as we do today.   Instead they planted three or four seeds in a small hill of soil.   As the corn grew, the Indians broke up the soil around the plants.   This got rid of weeds.

When the corn plants got bigger, the Indians would plant beans and squash in the same field as the corn.   They planted them between the hills of corn.   The bean vines would grow up the cornstalks.   The squash vines would spread out under the stalks.   In this way every bit of ground was used.

Preparing corn   The Indians cooked corn in many different ways. They would roast or boil the ears whole.   Sometimes they took the kernels off the cob and cooked them. Often they would grind precooked kernels into flour.   From the flour they made small round cakes.   They baked these in hot ashes.   At times they would add berries or pieces of dried deer meat to the flour.

Other foods   The Pennsylvania Indians also ate fish, such as shad and pike.   They caught fish in traps and with hooks, spears, and nets.   They hunted bear, deer, elk, and turkey. First they used spears for hunting.

Later they made bows and arrows. After the Europeans came, the Indians used guns that they had gotten from them.

The Indians ate hickory nuts, walnuts, chestnuts, and hazelnuts.   Apples, wild grapes, strawberries, raspberries, and blackberries were also favorites.

Before learning how to farm, the Indians gathered wild fruits and berries for food.

MAKING CORN CAKES

1. Taking the corn off the cob

2. Boiling the kernels

3. Grinding the cooked
   kernels into flour

4. Making cakes out of the
   flour and cooking them

Clothing   The Indians also had different kinds of clothing. Most of their clothing was made from deerskin. In the summer the men usually wore a short piece of clothing called a breech-cloth. The women wore a skirt that reached their knees and in cold weather usually a deerskin top. They often put beads on their clothing for decoration. When it got colder, both the men and the women would put on deerskin leggings. They would also wear robes made of bear, beaver, or raccoon fur. On their feet the Indians wore moccasins, which are special shoes made of deerskin.

Decorations were important to the Indians. Jewelry was made from shells, porcupine quills, or bits of deer antlers. Animal hair and feathers were also used. Men wore feathers in their hair. A person could tell what tribe an Indian was from by looking at these feathers. The Indians also made robes from feathers. These robes were worn mostly for celebrations. They were also good in the rain because the feathers shed water.

This museum display shows clothing that Iroquois women made of deerskin. It also shows some of the tools they used. Have you ever visited a museum? If so, what did you see?

Both men and women painted their faces. They often did this just for decoration. When the men went into battle, they would paint their faces and bodies so that they looked frightening.

Clans   The tribes of both the Algonquians and the Iroquois were divided into **clans.** A clan was a group of families who had a common ancestor. In Iroquois tribes, families in one clan would live together in a longhouse. The clans were named for animals. There might be a Turtle clan, a Wolf clan, and a Hawk clan. The animals were believed to be special ancestors and protectors of the clans.

Each clan had a council. The council governed, or ruled, the clan. Only men could belong to this council. The women of the clan, however, chose the members of the clan council. The clan councils sent people to speak for them at the tribal councils.

Government   Above the clan was the tribe. Each tribe had a chief. The Algonquian word for "chief" was **sachem** (sā′ chəm). A group of older men made up the tribal council, which helped the chief. In Iroquois tribes important women from the clans chose both the chief and the council members. The chief was in charge of the council meetings.

The silver earrings at the top were worn by Indian women. The comb at the bottom was made out of an animal bone.

The tribe was the most important group for the Algonquians. They did not have any group larger than the tribe. The Iroquois also lived in tribes. But, as you have read, some of the tribes were part of a larger group. These tribes, or nations, were joined together in a league. The league had a council. The main duty of the council was to keep peace among the nations. The members of the council were chosen by important women in the tribes.

Religion   The Indians believed that everything around them had life, or a spirit. Over everything was a chief god called the Great Spirit, or the Creator. He lived in the sky and watched over all things. Other gods helped him.

Religion was part of the Indians' everyday life. Good hunting, storms, sickness, and victory in battle were given to them by the Great Spirit. Once a year the Indians would come together for a special meeting known as the Big House Ceremony. They would build a house about 50 feet (15 m) long. For 12 days the Indians entered this house and prayed in different ways. They did this to thank the Great Spirit for all that he had given them during the year. Does this sound like a holiday that we have each year?

CHECKUP
1. Name four basic needs that all people have.
2. What is a clan?
3. Who was the chief god for the Indians?

3/CHAPTER REVIEW

Some Key Terms   On a piece of paper write the words missing from the sentences below. Use these words: *prehistory, maize, conservationist, longhouse, sachem.*

1. The Indians called corn _____ .
2. A _____ is the type of house the Iroquois built.
3. The story of a people before they learned to write things down is their _____ .
4. _____ is the Algonquian word for "chief."
5. A person who saves the environment and does not waste its gifts is a _____ .

Do Some Research   Use an encyclopedia or other reference book to find the answers to the following questions.
1. How did the Indians hunt animals?
2. How did the Indians travel around Pennsylvania?
3. Are there any Indian tribes in Pennsylvania today?

For Thought   Write a paragraph or two in answer to one of the following questions.
1. How can we know about the lives of the Indians if they did not write things down?
2. Why, do you think, did most of the Indians in Pennsylvania live between the Susquehanna and Delaware rivers?

4 Pennsylvania the Colony

Early Settlers in Pennsylvania

```
┌─ VOCABULARY ─────────────┐
  explorer        governor
  settler         capital
  settlement      flax
└──────────────────────────┘
```

The Dutch explore   The Indians were the first people to live in what is now Pennsylvania. Columbus arrived in America in 1492. After this, many countries in Europe sent **explorers** to America. An explorer is a person who looks for new things and new places. In 1616, an explorer from Holland named Cornelius Hendricksen sailed up the Delaware River. Holland is also called the Netherlands. The people who live in that country are called the Dutch. Hendricksen found another river that joins the Delaware River where the city of Philadelphia is today. He named this river the Schuyl-kill. The Dutch sent people to live along the two rivers. These people built forts and began to trade with the Indians for furs.

The Swedish arrive   Sometime later, Sweden became interested in sending **settlers** to the Delaware River area. Settlers are people who move to a new land to live. The place where they live is a **settlement.** In 1637, a Dutch explorer named Peter Minuit (min' ü it) sailed to America for Swe-den. He was sent to buy land from the Indians along the Delaware and Schuylkill rivers. This land would be a home for Swedish settlers. With two small ships, Minuit sailed up the Dela-ware River. He built a fort at the place on the river that is now Wilmington, Delaware. Minuit named it Fort Chris-tina after the young queen of Sweden. More Swedish settlers arrived 2 years later. But it was not until 1644 that a Swedish settlement was started in what is now Pennsylvania.

New Sweden   A **governor** for the Swedish settlement, Johan Printz, came to America in 1643. A governor is the most important leader of a settle-ment or state. One of the first things that Printz did was move the **capital** of

The painting on the next page is of the Swedish landing at Wilmington, Delaware. It can be seen at the American Swedish Historical Museum in Philadelphia.

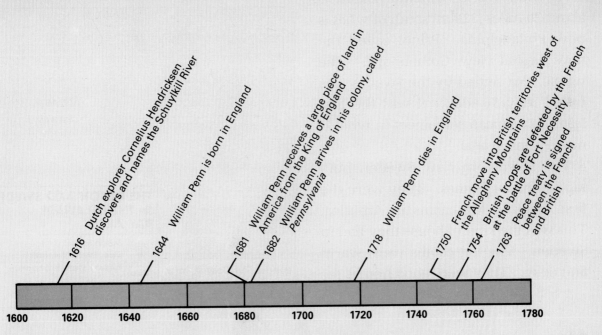

1616 Dutch explorer Cornelius Hendricksen discovers and names the Schuylkill River

1644 William Penn is born in England

1681 William Penn receives a large piece of land in America from the King of England

1682 William Penn arrives in his colony, called *Pennsylvania*

1718 William Penn dies in England

1750 French move into British territories west of the Allegheny Mountains

1754 British troops are defeated by the French at the battle of Fort Necessity

1763 Peace treaty is signed between the French and British

1600 1620 1640 1660 1680 1700 1720 1740 1760 1780

Johan Printz was a very big man. He weighed about 300 pounds.

the settlement from Fort Christina to Tinicum Island. A capital is the place where the leaders of a settlement, state, or country work. Tinicum Island is about 20 miles (32 km) south of what is now Philadelphia. Printz called the new capital New Gothenburg. The whole area settled by the Swedes was called New Sweden. It was the first lasting European settlement in what is now Pennsylvania.

The Swedes in New Sweden built log cabins for homes. They were the first to build log cabins in America. This was the kind of house they had in Sweden. The log cabins were warm and cozy. They were good homes for

the Swedes during the cold winters in America.

The Swedish settlers also began to farm the land. They were the first settlers to bring cattle to America for their farms. The Indians taught the Swedes how to grow corn, beans, and squash. They also planted **flax** and tobacco. Flax is a plant used to make linen cloth. Tobacco was an important crop because it was worth a lot of money in Europe.

The Dutch gain control The Swedish settlers began to have trouble with the Dutch. The Dutch felt that New Sweden really belonged to them, since they had explored the land and built forts there. In 1652 a small Dutch fort on the Delaware River named Fort Casimir was captured by the Swedes. This made the Dutch very angry.

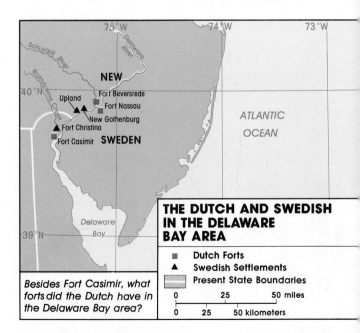

THE DUTCH AND SWEDISH IN THE DELAWARE BAY AREA

■ Dutch Forts
▲ Swedish Settlements
▢ Present State Boundaries

0   25   50 miles
0   25   50 kilometers

Besides Fort Casimir, what forts did the Dutch have in the Delaware Bay area?

This log cabin, built by Swedish settlers, can still be visited in Upper Darby, Pennsylvania. Are there any log cabins in your community?

Their governor, Peter Stuyvesant (stī′ ve sənt), sent an army to recapture the fort and to attack New Sweden. In 1655, the Swedes lost New Sweden to the Dutch. The Dutch let the Swedes stay on their farms if they wanted to. Most of the Swedish settlers stayed. But now they had to obey a Dutch governor.

England takes over   England also had settlements in America. The English had settled in what is now New England, Maryland, and Virginia. The Dutch lands, which now included New Sweden, were between these settlements. King Charles II of England wanted to join together the English set-

tlements. In 1664, he sent a large army to attack the Dutch. The Dutch surrendered, or gave up. In this way, the English took control of the Dutch and Swedish settlements. These settlements included the area that is now New York State and the land along the Delaware River. The English capital was moved to Upland, which is now the city of Chester in Pennsylvania.

CHECKUP

1. What was the first lasting European settlement in what is now Pennsylvania?
2. Name two things that the Swedish were the first to bring to America.
3. Why did the English attack the Dutch in 1664?

William Penn and His Colony

Penn and the Quakers   Can you imagine what it would be like to live in a place where everyone had to follow the same religion? Many countries in Europe used to be such places. In England the Church of England was the *official* church. It was the only religion that English people were supposed to follow. That was the law. People who followed other religions were treated badly and were even sometimes put in jail.

William Penn was made the owner of his colony by the King of England. He also served as the colony's governor.

A young man named William Penn did not want to follow the official religion. Penn had been born in England in 1644. His father was Sir William Penn, a famous admiral in the king's navy. When young Penn went to college, he learned about a new religion. The members of the religion were called the Society of Friends, or **Quakers.** They believed that all people should live as friends. They said that all people were equal in the eyes of God. It did not matter if you were rich or poor. The Quakers were against war and would not fight. They lived and worshiped in a simple way. They did not worship in churches or have ministers.

Penn became a Quaker when he was 23 years old. Because of this, he had to leave college. Only students who belonged to the Church of England could go to the college. Penn's father was angry with him for this. But this did not stop Penn from becoming an important Quaker leader. He went to jail many times for his beliefs.

Land in America for the Quakers Admiral Penn died in 1670. He left all his wealth and property to his son, William. When he was alive, Admiral Penn had loaned a large sum of money to the king. Now the king owed the money to William.

Many Quakers found a better life in Pennsylvania.

When the king could not repay the money, Penn asked him for land in America. Penn wanted a place where Quakers and others could live and worship without fear. On March 4, 1681, the king gave Penn all the land in America between 39 and 42 degrees of north latitude. It was to stretch to the west from the Delaware River for 5 degrees of longitude. Penn wanted to call the land Sylvania, which means "woods." The king wanted to name the land after Admiral Penn. In the end it was called Pennsylvania, or "Penn's Woods."

Penn arrives in Pennsylvania

William Penn arrived in his **colony** on October 29, 1682, with over 100 other Quakers. A colony is land that is settled by people who leave their own country but remain citizens of that country. Before coming to Pennsylvania, Penn wrote a **constitution** for the colony. A constitution is a set of laws by which a place is governed. Pennsylvania's constitution set up a Provincial Council to make laws for the colony and a General Assembly to approve the laws.

Pennsylvania's first set of laws was called the Great Law. The Great Law gave freedom of religion to everyone in the colony. This meant that all people in the colony could worship in their own way. It made the Dutch and Swedes in the colony English citizens. The Great Law showed the respect that the Quakers had for people and their rights.

Land for sale   One of the first things that Penn did in his colony was to make peace with the Indians. Even though the king had given him Pennsylvania, Penn still paid the Indians for the land. Penn and the Indians met many times. They signed land and peace treaties with each other.

Then Penn began to sell his land. He knew that many people in England and other European countries would buy it. He sold it in small pieces at low prices so that many people could own land. Many people bought the land. The whole colony grew quickly. There were three counties in the colony—Bucks, Chester, and Philadelphia counties.

Penn had made plans for the city of Philadelphia while he was still in England. He had laid it out as the capital of the colony. It was already growing. Other Quakers moved in and around the city. Work was started on a country home for Penn on the Delaware River. The home would be called Pennsbury Manor.

William Penn wanted to treat the Indians fairly. Here, Penn and other Quaker settlers are trading goods with the Indians in return for land.

Pennsbury Manor, the home of William Penn, is located in Bucks County. What does Penn's home tell you about his lifestyle?

Other people come to Penn's colony Other people besides the English came to Pennsylvania. Many were Germans who wanted freedom of religion. German Quakers bought land on the northwest edge of Philadelphia. They named this place Germantown. Two other German groups settled in what is now Lancaster County. They were the Mennonites (me′ nə nītz) and the Amish (äm′ ish). The Moravians, (mə rāv′ ē ənz), another German group, also came.

People from Scotland came to Pennsylvania to settle. They were called the Scotch-Irish because they had lived in Ireland for a while. The Scotch-Irish had come to Pennsylvania looking for religious freedom. They also wanted to buy land. The Scotch-Irish settled farther west than the German groups. They even crossed the Allegheny Mountains.

Many other people came to the colony. Among them were Jews, Catholics, and other Protestants. No colony had as great a mix of people as Pennsylvania.

Hannah Penn, the wife of William Penn, governed Pennsylvania after the death of her husband.

The Pennsylvania Dutch

Between the years 1683 and 1806, many people came to Pennsylvania from Germany. These Germans were given the name *Pennsylvania Dutch*. The reason that they received this incorrect nickname was due to a misunderstanding. The German word for their own language is *Deutsch,* which is pronounced *doich.* Other settlers in Pennsylvania thought they were saying "Dutch," and therefore thought the language they were speaking was Dutch. Because of this, these German settlers were called Dutch.

The Germans came to Pennsylvania in two large groups. These were known as the Church Germans and the "plain" Germans. Church Germans belonged to the Lutheran and Reformed churches. "Plain" Germans included groups such as the Mennonites, Moravians, and Amish. The Moravians settled the towns of Nazareth and Bethlehem in eastern Pennsylvania. The Mennonites and the Amish moved into Berks, Lancaster, and Lebanon counties. These people came to Pennsylvania looking for religious freedom.

The Amish are the most famous of the "plain" Germans. The group is named after its founder in Europe, Jacob Ammann. The Amish believe in following the teachings of the Bible very strictly.

Amish life revolves around religion. Every other Sunday the Amish gather in the home of one of their members for a worship service. It usually lasts for 3 hours.

The Amish are excellent farmers. They believe in living a very simple life, without the use of modern conveniences. For example, the Amish use horse-drawn plows rather than modern tractors. Also, the Amish do not use cars or telephones. Though they lack modern farming methods, the Amish farms in Lancaster County are among the most productive in the state.

Many of Pennsylvania's early settlers were farmers. This painting shows what Bethlehem, Pennsylvania looked like in 1757. Bethlehem was settled by German immigrants.

Penn's family takes over   Penn had to go back to England in 1702. He never returned to Pennsylvania. He died in England on July 30, 1718. His wife, Hannah, took care of the colony after he died. She was the only woman to govern Pennsylvania. After she died, Penn's sons ran the colony.

CHECKUP

1. What is the Society of Friends?
2. What groups came to settle in Pennsylvania?
3. Who ran the colony after William Penn died?

Life in the Colony

┌─ **VOCABULARY** ─────────────────┐
| hemp | gristmill |
| linsey-woolsey | Conestoga wagon |
└──────────────────────────────────┘

Farming   Most people came to Pennsylvania to farm. This was hard work because Pennsylvania had thick forests. Farmers had to cut the trees down or burn them. Then they had to dig out the stumps. Only after this could they plow the soil and plant crops.

PHILADELPHIA AROUND 1760

Buildings
Burial Grounds
Parks

0   ¼ mile
0   ¼ kilometers

The Quakers were very active in Philadelphia. Find Friends Schoolhouse, Almshouse, and three Friends Meetings on this map.

The first crop planted was usually corn. It grew well on the newly cleared land. The early farmers also found that wheat grew well in Pennsylvania. People in the other colonies were willing to pay a lot of money for wheat. For over 100 years, Pennsylvania was the leading producer of wheat in America.

Farmers also grew other crops, such as flax and **hemp.** The flax was made into linen. The linen was sometimes mixed with wool to make a cloth called **linsey-woolsey.** The fibers of the hemp plant made very strong rope.

Philadelphia   Philadelphia grew quickly. It had been built on the Delaware River and was an important port. A port is a place where ships come to unload and load their goods. Goods from the colonies and from England were shipped through Philadelphia. This trade made Philadelphia the richest city in the colonies.

In 1700, over 5,000 people lived in Philadelphia. By 1750, it had almost 18,000 people and was the largest city in the colonies. Many beautiful brick buildings were built along its straight streets. The city also had many fine parks.

Philadelphia was also the center for the arts in the colonies. Benjamin West painted there. Francis Hopkinson made the city come alive with his music. There were plays to go to and interesting newspapers and magazines to read.

How the towns grew   As time passed, other towns began to appear in Pennsylvania. Farmers needed a place to sell their goods. The places where they met became small towns. Soon blacksmiths, shoemakers, and other craftworkers began to do business in the towns. Lancaster was laid out in 1730. Reading, Easton, and York followed.

One of the most important businesses near the new towns was the **gristmill.** A gristmill was a large building where the farmers' wheat and other grains were ground into flour. Inside the mill a big round stone turned around and did the grinding. The stone was connected to a wheel outside the building. Water from a stream or river ran over the wheel and turned it. When the wheel turned, the grinding stone did its job. Sometimes a saw blade was connected to a water wheel. The blade could cut logs into boards, or lumber. A mill where lumber is cut is called a sawmill.

The turning water wheel provided the power to make the grinding stone in the gristmill and the saw blade in the sawmill do their jobs.

Ironmaking   Another industry started near the towns. This was ironmaking. Pennsylvania was rich in wood, limestone, and iron ore. It soon became the leading ironmaking colony in America.

Moving west   The good farming and the growing industry in Pennsylvania brought more and more people to the colony. It was not long before more land was needed. Larger sections of land were bought from the Indians. By 1775, the colony of Pennsylvania was almost as large as the state of Pennsylvania is today.

The people who came looking for land had to move farther west. People began to cross the Allegheny Mountains. First, trappers and hunters crossed the mountains. Soon traders followed. They traded with the hunters and trappers for furs. They also traded with the Indians. Some of them built trading posts. Farmers followed the traders.

As settlers moved west, they faced a problem. The trails west were very rough. How were they going to carry all of their belongings to their new homes in the west? Farmers also wondered how they were going to get their goods to market.

The answer to this problem came from Lancaster County. A new kind of

The Conestoga Wagon helped colonists cross the Allegheny Mountains to settle in western Pennsylvania.

wagon had been invented there. This new wagon was first used by the Pennsylvania Germans to carry their goods to Philadelphia. It was about 16 feet (5 m) long, 4 feet (1 m) wide, and 4 feet (1 m) deep. A canvas top stretched over wooden hoops covered it. The wagon rode on four large wooden wheels. These had bands of iron like tires around the rims. The wagon could carry 2,500 to 3,500 pounds (1,135 to 1,589 kg) of material. Because the wagon was first made in the Conestoga (kän ə stō′ gə) Valley, it was called a **Conestoga wagon.**

CHECKUP

1. What crop brought the early farmers in Pennsylvania a lot of money?
2. What was linsey-woolsey?
3. How much weight could a Conestoga wagon carry?

The French and Indian War

— VOCABULARY —
bastion

Problems with the French   The French had come to North America before the English, or British. The first French settlements in North America were in Canada. Many Frenchmen came to North America to become fur traders. By 1750, the French were moving from Canada into the lands west of the Allegheny Mountains. They said that these lands belonged to France. They began to build forts from Lake Erie to the Ohio River. Among them were Fort Presque Isle, Fort LeBoeuf, and Fort Machault. Find the French forts on the map on this page.

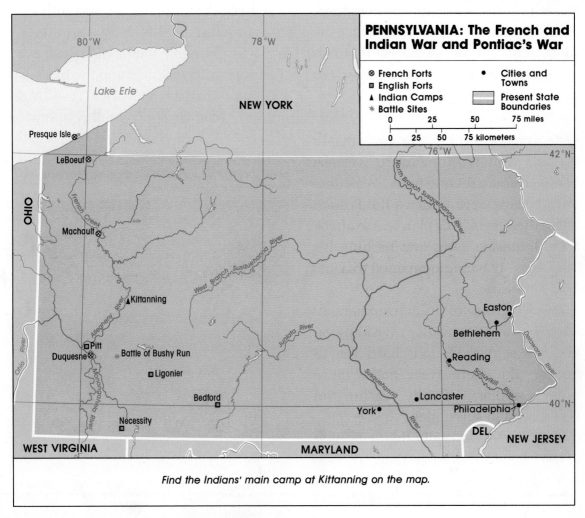

PENNSYLVANIA: The French and Indian War and Pontiac's War

- ⊗ French Forts
- ▣ English Forts
- ▲ Indian Camps
- ✳ Battle Sites
- • Cities and Towns
- Present State Boundaries

0   25   50   75 miles
0   25   50   75 kilometers

Find the Indians' main camp at Kittanning on the map.

The British warn the French   The British believed that the lands west of the Alleghenies were theirs. Pennsylvania and other British colonies claimed the lands west of the mountains. Virginia was one of the colonies that claimed these lands. In 1753, the governor of Virginia sent George Washington to Fort LeBoeuf to tell the French to leave. The French refused. After Washington left with their answer, the French built the largest of their forts, Fort Duquesne. It was built where the Allegheny and Monongahela (mə nän gə hē′ lə) rivers meet and form the Ohio River.

War breaks out   The governor of Virginia sent Washington to western Pennsylvania a second time. Washington's orders were to drive the French out of their forts. His plan was to attack Fort Duquesne. But first he built his own fort. Washington named this fort Fort Necessity.

A large group of French soldiers attacked Fort Necessity. Washington and his soldiers fought hard for 10 hours. But there were many more French soldiers. Finally Washington was forced to surrender.

This battle was really the beginning of the French and Indian War. On one side were Great Britain and its 13 American colonies. On the other side were France and most of the Indian groups.

Braddock's defeat   In 1755, Great Britain sent an army to drive the French from the western lands. The commander of this army was General Edward Braddock. He and his British soldiers set out to capture Fort Duquesne. George Washington and a number of Virginia soldiers were with him.

Braddock reached the Monongahela River on July 9, 1755. He was only 7 miles (11 km) from Fort Duquesne. It was here that the French and Indians attacked him and his army. Braddock was a brave man. But he did not know that the French soldiers and the Indians fought in a different way. They hid behind trees to shoot at the enemy.

The French surprised the British troops led by General Braddock. During the surprise attack, Braddock was wounded and later died from his wounds.

The British soldiers dressed in bright red uniforms. They marched in the open in straight lines. It was easy for the French and Indians to surprise the British. Braddock was wounded in the battle, and later died from the wounds. The British were defeated.

The capture of Fort Duquesne
In England, William Pitt was put in charge of the war plans. In 1758, he sent General John Forbes to Philadelphia with an army. He was to capture Fort Duquesne. When Forbes became ill, Colonel Henry Bouquet (boo kā′) took over for him.

Bouquet marched west across Pennsylvania. Washington joined him with a group of Virginians. They reached the fort on November 25, 1758. The night before, the French had set fire to the fort and left. The British decided to build a new fort. They were afraid that the French might come back. The fort was called Fort Pitt for William Pitt.

A fort with five sides was built. Usually forts had four sides. At the points where the walls met, small towers called **bastions** (bas′ tē ənz) were built. These helped in defending the walls. Outside the walls of the fort, rings of ditches, more walls, and mounds of dirt were made. The three rivers also protected the fort. Strong

The British troops, led by George Washington, raise the British flag at Fort Duquesne. Capturing this fort helped the British win the French and Indian War.

buildings of brick were built inside the fort. The fort covered 18 acres (7 ha) of land. It was the largest and strongest fort in the west.

Great Britain wins the war More British victories followed. At last the French surrendered. Great Britain and France signed a peace treaty in 1763. The French agreed to give up Canada and all the lands west of the Allegheny Mountains as far as the Mississippi River.

Pontiac's war The fighting between the British and the Indians went on. Indian tribes attacked British settlements in western Pennsylvania. Pontiac, a chief of the Ottawa Indians, led the attacks. Pontiac began these attacks in June 1763. One after another, the British forts fell to the Indians. Only Fort Ligonier, Fort Bedford, and Fort Pitt held out. Colonel Bouquet set out from Philadelphia for Fort Pitt with an army to stop Pontiac.

Bouquet reached Bushy Run, about 20 miles (32 km) east of Fort Pitt, in August. The Indians attacked him. The battle lasted all day. Bouquet and his men were outnumbered and surrounded. Finally, Bouquet ordered some of his men to pull away. The Indians thought all of the British were

Pontiac was a chief of the Ottawa Indians. He led raids against British settlements in western Pennsylvania.

Colonel Henry Bouquet led the British army to victory at the Battle of Bushy Run.

leaving and ran out to capture them. Bouquet and his men were then able to fire on the Indians. The Indians fled. In 1764, the war with the Indians came to an end.

CHECKUP

1. Why did the British send a warning to the French?
2. How did the governor of Pennsylvania stop the Indian raids?
3. Who led the army that captured Fort Duquesne and defeated the Indians at Bushy Run?

4/CHAPTER REVIEW

Some Key Terms On a piece of paper write the words missing from the sentences below. Use these words: *settlers, constitution, linsey-woolsey, Conestoga wagon,* and *bastions.*

1. _____ was a kind of cloth made out of linen and wool.
2. People who move to a new land to live are called _____ .
3. Small towers at the corners of a fort are called _____ .
4. A _____ is a set of laws by which a place is governed.
5. The _____ was first used by the Pennsylvania Germans.

Do Some Research Use an encyclopedia or other reference book to find the answers to the following questions.

1. Who were William Penn's sons?
2. What was the Walking Purchase?
3. What peace treaty ended the French and Indian War?

For Thought Write a paragraph or two in answer to one of the following questions.

1. What important ideas were included in Pennsylvania's early laws?
2. How did the gristmill and the iron furnace help towns grow?
3. Why was it important to control the place where the French built Fort Duquesne?

Problems with Great Britain

VOCABULARY

congress	patriot
repeal	Declaration of
representative	Independence

The Stamp Act   The French and Indian War had cost Great Britain a lot of money. Money was needed to protect the lands the British had won in America. To raise money, King George III decided to make the American colonies pay new taxes. The king felt that the Americans should pay their share because the British victory had helped the colonies.

In 1765, the British government passed the Stamp Act. The Stamp Act said that the colonists had to buy tax stamps. These stamps had to be placed on newspapers, marriage licenses, calendars, and even playing cards. This made the colonists angry. They held a **congress** in New York to talk about the new taxes. A congress is a meeting

people have to discuss ideas or problems. The meeting was known as the Stamp Act Congress. John Dickinson of Pennsylvania wrote down the complaints of the colonists. His two papers, "Declaration of Rights" and "Petition to the King," said that the American colonists should not have to obey tax laws that they did not help make.

In 1766, Great Britain was forced to **repeal,** or take back, the Stamp Act. This meant that the Stamp Act was no longer a law.

The Townshend Acts   Great Britain still needed to raise money. In 1767, it passed the Townshend Acts. These laws said that Americans had to pay taxes on goods from Great Britain. Some of these goods were paint, glass, paper, lead, and tea. Anyone who did not pay these taxes would be punished.

The colonists refused to buy the taxed goods. John Dickinson again wrote about the colonists' feelings. In his "Letters from a Farmer in Pennsylvania," he wrote that the taxes were unfair. In 1770, Great Britain repealed most of the Townshend Acts.

Colonists, angered by the Stamp Act, often treated agents who sold the stamps very badly. Here some agents, tarred and feathered, are paraded through the streets.

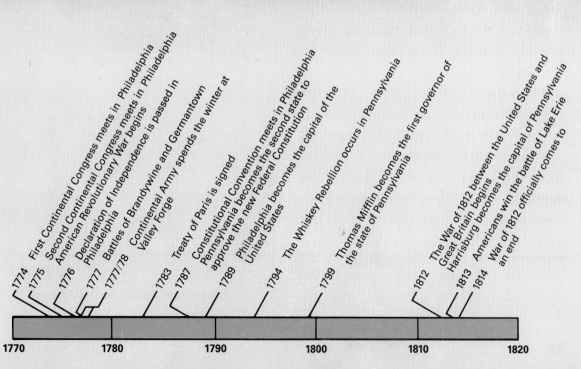

1774 First Continental Congress meets in Philadelphia
1775 Second Continental Congress meets in Philadelphia
1776 American Revolutionary War begins
 Declaration of Independence is passed in
 Philadelphia
1777 Battles of Brandywine and Germantown
1777/78 Continental Army spends the winter at
 Valley Forge
1783 Treaty of Paris is signed
1787 Constitutional Convention meets in Philadelphia
 Pennsylvania becomes the second state to
 approve the new Federal Constitution
1789 Philadelphia becomes the capital of the
 United States
1794 The Whiskey Rebellion occurs in Pennsylvania
1799 Thomas Mifflin becomes the first governor of
 the state of Pennsylvania
1812 The War of 1812 between the United States and
 Great Britain begins
 Harrisburg becomes the capital of Pennsylvania
1813 Americans win the battle of Lake Erie
1814 War of 1812 officially comes to
 an end

1770   1780   1790   1800   1810   1820

The First Continental Congress
The colonists were angry that Great Britain passed laws without listening to them. There was no one in the British government who spoke for them. **Representatives** from the colonies held a meeting at Carpenters' Hall in Philadelphia in September 1774. A representative is someone people choose to speak for them. Philadelphia was chosen as the meeting place because it was in the center of the colonies. It was also the leading city in America. The meeting was known as the First Continental Congress.

Pennsylvania sent seven representatives to the Continental Congress. John Dickinson was also there. He was asked again to write about the colonists' complaints. The colonists wanted King George to repeal all the unfair laws. They also wanted to have all the rights and freedoms they were supposed to have as British citizens. This message was sent to the king. He never sent an answer.

When the First Continental Congress ended in October, its members went home. They tried to get other colonists to stop buying British goods. They also spoke out against the unfair taxes. The members of the First Continental Congress and others who were against the unfair control of the colonies by Great Britain were known as **patriots.**

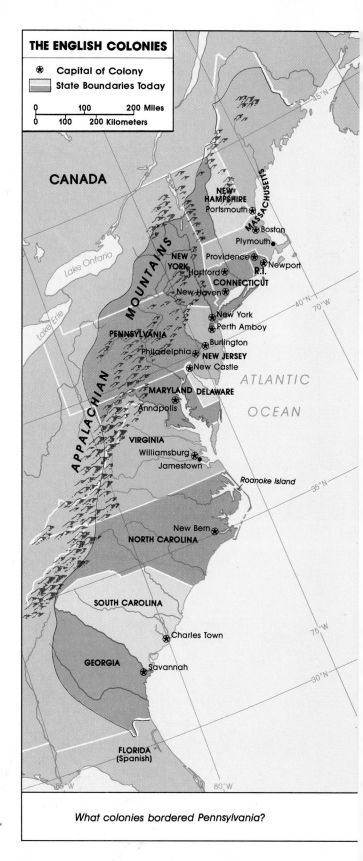

THE ENGLISH COLONIES

⊛ Capital of Colony

State Boundaries Today

0   100   200 Miles
0 100   200 Kilometers

CANADA

Lake Ontario

Lake Erie

NEW HAMPSHIRE
Portsmouth

MASSACHUSETTS

Boston

Plymouth

NEW YORK
Providence
Hartford
Newport

R.I.

CONNECTICUT
New Haven

MOUNTAINS

New York

Perth Amboy

PENNSYLVANIA
Burlington

Philadelphia   NEW JERSEY
New Castle

ATLANTIC

APPALACHIAN

MARYLAND DELAWARE

OCEAN

Annapolis

VIRGINIA
Williamsburg
Jamestown

Roanoke Island

New Bern

NORTH CAROLINA

SOUTH CAROLINA

Charles Town

GEORGIA   Savannah

FLORIDA
(Spanish)

What colonies bordered Pennsylvania?

Franklin and Adams helped Jefferson (standing) write the Declaration of Independence.

The Declaration of Independence   In April of 1775, fighting broke out between the Americans and British. Shots were fired at the British in the towns of Lexington and Concord in the colony of Massachusetts.

About a month later the Second Continental Congress met in the building now known as Independence Hall in Philadelphia. The Continental Congress decided to raise a Continental army to fight the British. George Washington was chosen to lead the army. A year later the Continental Congress began to discuss the idea of forming a new nation. The nation would be independent of Great Britain. When the idea was put to a vote, it passed. Three men from Pennsylvania voted for the idea. They were Benjamin Franklin, John Morton, and James Wilson.

A group of five men, including Franklin, worked together to prepare a paper to be sent to Great Britain. Thomas Jefferson of Virginia wrote the paper. It was called the **Declaration of Independence.** It said that the colonies were now free from Great Britain. It also named the new nation the United States of America. On July 4, 1776, the members of the Continental Congress passed the Declaration of Independence. Philadelphia was made the first capital of the new nation.

CHECKUP

1. What was the Stamp Act?
2. What did John Dickinson do at the Stamp Act Congress and the First Continental Congress?
3. What did the Declaration of Independence say?

63

The War for Independence

The early war years   The Declaration of Independence was only the beginning. Now the War for Independence had to be fought and won. The War for Independence is sometimes also called the Revolutionary War. The war did not go well for the Americans at first. Washington's army was small and poorly trained. The American navy was also very small. The British had a strong army and the best navy in the world.

The fighting that had begun in New England spread to New York, New Jersey, and the other colonies. In December 1776, Washington and his army had to leave New Jersey. They crossed the Delaware River to Pennsylvania. On Christmas night the Americans recrossed the Delaware and attacked a camp of **Hessians** (hesh' ənz) at Trenton, New Jersey. The Hessians were soldiers from Germany who were hired to fight for the British. The American army captured 900 Hessians.

"Washington Crossing the Delaware" is one of the most famous paintings of the Revolutionary War. It was done in the early 1800s by Emmanuel Leutze, a German artist.

The Metropolitan Museum of Art, Gift of John Stewart Kennedy, 1897.

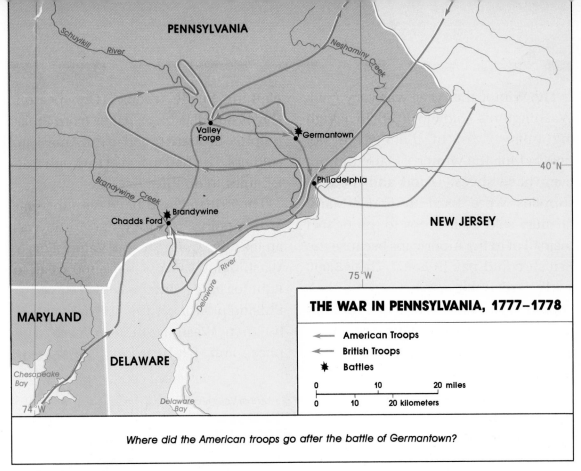

THE WAR IN PENNSYLVANIA, 1777–1778

- ← American Troops
- ← British Troops
- ✳ Battles

| 0 | 10 | 20 miles |
| 0 | 10 | 20 kilometers |

Where did the American troops go after the battle of Germantown?

This battle, known as the battle of Trenton, was the first great victory for the Americans in the war.

The war came to Pennsylvania in 1777. The British wanted to capture Philadelphia. British troops landed in Maryland and marched north toward Philadelphia. On September 11, the British met Washington and his troops at Chadds Ford, one of the crossings of Brandywine Creek. This was the battle of Brandywine. The Americans fought hard. Edward Hector was a hero on that day. He was one of many blacks who fought in the Continental army. When the order came to move back, Hector drove a wagon over the battlefield. He gathered and saved hundreds of guns for the army. But the Americans lost this battle and the battle that followed at Germantown. The British reached Philadelphia 2 weeks later.

Valley Forge The Continental Congress left Philadelphia for Lancaster and then York. Many other patriots in Philadelphia also left before the British arrived. The British stayed in and around Philadelphia. Washington and his army had to find a place to camp for the winter. The place he chose was Valley Forge, about 20 miles (32 km) from Philadelphia. From there he could keep watch on the movements of the British army.

The winter that year was very cold. Washington's soldiers lived in rough log huts. Most of them were not dressed for the winter. Many did not even have shoes. Food and medical supplies were hard to find. Many farmers sold their crops to the British instead of to the Americans because the British could pay in gold. Over 3,000 soldiers died that winter.

More would have died if it had not been for the deeds of some brave men and women. They brought food and clothing to the troops. One person, Cyrus Bustill, a black baker from Philadelphia, brought bread to the American soldiers. He had to travel through British lines to do this.

The British could have won the war at this point. All they had to do was attack the Americans at Valley Forge. Washington's troops were too weak to fight for long. But the British stayed in Philadelphia until the spring of 1778. By then Washington had food, supplies, and fresh troops. His army

Washington reviews his troops during the terrible winter of 1777–1778 at Valley Forge. What thoughts, do you suppose, were in the minds of the parading soldiers?

began to exercise daily. When they left Valley Forge in June, they were a tough, well-trained group of soldiers.

During this time the French had been helping the Americans secretly with money and supplies. In the spring of 1778 they joined the Americans in openly fighting the British. Benjamin Franklin had gone to France early that year for help. The French agreed to send an army and a **fleet.** A fleet is a group of ships sailing together. The British left Philadelphia when they heard that France was helping the Americans.

Fighting on the frontier   Fighting with the British was also going on on the **frontier** of Pennsylvania. A frontier is land that is on the edge of unsettled country. Most of the Indians in Pennsylvania had chosen to fight on the side of the British. Attacks on the Indians and the British from Fort Pitt began to be successful for the Americans. Under the command of General John Sullivan and Colonel Daniel Brodhead, American soldiers won many battles against the Iroquois. By the end of 1779, the Indians were only able to carry out small raids on the Americans.

Final victory   In 1781, Great Britain sent a large army to Virginia. General Cornwallis was its commander. After

General John Sullivan of New Hampshire led the troops defending the Pennsylvania frontier.

raiding central Virginia, Cornwallis moved his army to Yorktown. Washington saw a chance to trap Cornwallis and his troops there. With the help of the French army and fleet, the Americans were able to surround the British. Together the Americans and the French had 16,000 soldiers. Cornwallis only had 7,000. After fighting for weeks, the British surrendered on October 19, 1781. This was the last great battle of the war.

Pennsylvania's part in the war

Pennsylvania played an important part in the Revolutionary War. Perhaps you have heard Pennsylvania called the Keystone State. In an arch made of stone, the keystone is the center stone. The center stone has a special shape that helps hold the other stones of the arch together. Pennsylvania was like a keystone. It was in the center of the new nation.

Pennsylvania was a strong keystone during the War for Independence. The people of Pennsylvania did many things to help in the war. Many of them joined the army. Thirteen **regiments** (rej′ ə mənts) came from the state. A regiment is a part of an army. These regiments fought in many battles under General Anthony Wayne. They were sometimes called the Pennsylvania Line. Women from Pennsylvania also did their part during the Revolutionary War. They managed farms and shops while their husbands, brothers, and fathers fought the British. Other women followed the army. They washed, cooked, and sewed for the soldiers. Others nursed the sick and the wounded.

Women played a big part in America's struggle for freedom. Here 16-year-old Sibyl Ludington rallies townspeople to go turn back an invading British force.

Molly Pitcher

During America's Revolutionary War, many women from Pennsylvania helped the Continental army. Some made clothing and bandages for the troops. Others helped to prepare meals. Some cared for the wounded. Some women even fought in battle. One woman who fought in a battle was named Mary Ludwig Hays.

Mary Ludwig was born in Trenton, New Jersey, in 1754. She married John Caspar Hays and moved with her husband to Carlisle, Pennsylvania. When John joined the Continental army, Mary went with him. At the battle of Monmouth (near present-day Freehold, New Jersey) in June 1778, Mary carried pitchers of water to the American soldiers. Throughout the hot summer day, cries of "Molly, bring the pitcher!" were heard on the battlefield. Because of this, Mary received the nickname Molly Pitcher.

During the battle, John Hays was wounded. Molly then took over her husband's cannon for the rest of the battle. After the battle, George Washington made Molly an honorary lieutenant in the Continental army. In 1822, the Pennsylvania legislature honored Molly by giving her a military pension because of her bravery. Molly Pitcher died in 1832.

Pennsylvania gave tons of supplies to the troops. The farms provided horses and food. Samuel Wetherill, a clothmaker, supplied uniforms for the soldiers. The iron furnaces produced iron. It was used to make cannons, cannonballs, swords, and muskets. Most of the gunpowder used by the army came from Pennsylvania. Ships for the navy were built on the Delaware River at Philadelphia.

When money was a problem for America during the war, Pennsylvanians helped out. Two men worked especially hard to raise money. Robert Morris urged France and Holland to lend America large sums of money. Haym Salomon used his own money to help America. Pennsylvanians truly helped win the War for Independence.

The treaty of Paris   It took the British and the Americans almost two years to agree on the terms of the peace treaty. On September 3, 1783, the British and the Americans signed a peace treaty called the **Treaty of Paris.** It was called that because it was signed in Paris, France. The treaty said that the United States of America was a free nation. It was free from Great Britain. The treaty also gave the United States all the land between the Atlantic Ocean and the Mississippi River, from Canada to Florida.

CHECKUP
1. Who were the Hessians?
2. Where did Washington spend the winter of 1777 – 1778?
3. Where was the last great battle of the Revolutionary War?

At Cornwall, north of Lancaster, iron was produced in this building called the Cornwall Furnace. The inset shows the actual furnace inside the building.

A New Nation Is Born

─ VOCABULARY ─

Constitutional Convention ratify

The Constitutional Convention
Now that the United States was a free nation, it needed a constitution. As you remember, a constitution is a set of laws by which a place is governed. In the spring of 1787, representatives from the states met again in Independence Hall in Philadelphia to write a constitution. The meeting was called the **Constitutional Convention.** George Washington was the leader of the convention. Benjamin Franklin led the group from Pennsylvania. Other important Pennsylvanians at the convention were James Wilson and Gouverneur Morris.

Today, many people visit Independence Hall.

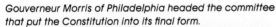

Gouverneur Morris of Philadelphia headed the committee that put the Constitution into its final form.

The representatives worked all through the summer. Many of Wilson's ideas went into the Constitution. Morris was asked to draw up the final copy of the Constitution. Under the Constitution there would be a President. There would also be a group called the Congress to make laws. The Supreme Court would interpret, or explain, the laws.

Adopting the Constitution The Constitution was finished on September 17, 1787. Nine of the 13 states had to **ratify,** or approve, it before it could be put into use. The Pennsylvania Assembly called a meeting to ratify the Constitution. James Wilson spoke strongly in favor of it. In December 1787, Pennsylvania became the second state to approve the Constitution. Other states followed.

Thomas Mifflin was Pennsylvania's first governor.

The Constitution became the law of the land in 1788. George Washington was chosen as the first President. The capital of the nation was moved to New York. But it was moved back to Philadelphia a year later. Philadelphia was the nation's capital until 1800, when the government moved to Washington, D.C.

Pennsylvania's government

In 1790, Thomas Mifflin, a Revolutionary War hero from Pennsylvania, became the first governor of the state. The state capital was moved to Lancaster. In 1812, it was moved to Harrisburg because people wanted a capital closer to the center of the state. Harrisburg has been the capital of Pennsylvania since then.

CHECKUP

1. Where was the Constitutional Convention held?
2. When did Pennsylvania ratify the Constitution of the United States?
3. Who was the first governor of the state of Pennsylvania?

Growth and Problems

Pennsylvania grows   One of the first things the state of Pennsylvania did was buy the land owned by the family of William Penn. The state also tried to get more people to move west. To do this, it began to sell land there in 1784. The land did not cost much. For a time it was sold for only 10 cents an acre. Many people had already settled on land in western Pennsylvania. These people were given first right to buy the land they had been living on. All they had to do was show that they had made that land better.

In 1792, Pennsylvania settled an old argument over a piece of land in the northwest, along Lake Erie. This piece of land, which was shaped like a triangle, was called the **Erie Triangle.** The states of Massachusetts, New York, and Pennsylvania all claimed the Erie Triangle. When New York and Massachusetts gave up their claims to the land, Pennsylvania bought the land from the United States. A town called Erie was built there to serve as a port on the lake. After this land was bought, Pennsylvania took on the size and shape it has today.

The town of Pittsburgh   The settlement around Fort Pitt grew a great deal in the years after the war. Soon the settlement had grown into a new town called Pittsburgh. Because it was located where the Allegheny and Monongahela rivers meet and form the Ohio River, the town quickly became a trading center. Many settlers moving west passed through Pittsburgh.

Iron was plentiful in the area around the town. Pittsburgh quickly became a manufacturing center. Iron furnaces began to produce large amounts of

In the late 1700s, Pittsburgh, a busy river port, became a center for building wooden boats and barges.

Pittsburgh is still the center of Pennsylvania's important steel-making industry.

iron. Glass was also made in Pittsburgh. In the late 1700s, there were as many furnaces making glass as there were making iron in the town. Pittsburgh also became a center for building boats and barges. With all the trade on the rivers, many boats and barges were needed. Because of the forests around the town and the iron being made there, Pittsburgh was a good place to build these things. By 1800, there were about 1,500 people living in Pittsburgh.

Farmers rebel   Although manufacturing was becoming important in Pittsburgh, most of the people in the western part of the state were farmers. A farming life was not easy in western Pennsylvania. In 1791, farmers in the western part of the state began to have more problems.

In that year the United States government placed a tax on whiskey to raise money that it needed. This tax was hard on the farmers of western Pennsylvania. They made a lot of whiskey from the corn they grew. It was easier for them to ship barrels of whiskey over the mountains than sacks of corn. The corn sometimes got wet and spoiled. Often the animals carrying the corn ate it on the trip. The farmers were angry about the whiskey tax. They said that it was as bad as the British taxes had been.

A group of farmers who lived just south of Pittsburgh got together to rebel, or fight, against the tax. James McFarlane led the group. The farmers attacked the home of General John Neville, who was in charge of collecting the tax in the region. They burned his home to the ground.

The rebellion ended when President Washington sent troops to the area in September 1794. This rebellion is known as the **Whiskey Rebellion.** It was one of the first tests of the new national government.

In the 1790s, farmers in western Pennsylvania rebelled against a tax on whiskey. Here, a tax collector has been tarred and feathered. Do you think such action was right?

"We have met the enemy and they are ours." With these words, Commodore Oliver Hazard Perry reported the American victory over the British fleet at the battle of Lake Erie.

The War of 1812 Great Britain and France had been at war since 1793. America joined the war against Great Britain in 1812. It did this because Great Britain was making it hard for the United States to trade with countries in Europe. British ships stopped American ships on the Atlantic Ocean.

America fought against the British from 1812 to 1815. One battle took place in Pennsylvania. The British wanted to gain control of the Great Lakes. During the summer of 1813, Oliver Hazard Perry, an American naval officer, went to the port of Erie. There he had a fleet of eight ships built. Workers from all over Pennsylvania came to build the ships. Black and white sailors from the state served on the ships. On September 10, 1813, Perry and his fleet fought the British on Lake Erie. After a long and bloody battle, the Americans won.

In 1814, the British captured and burned Washington, D.C. Philadelphians feared an attack on their city was next. Although the British never marched on Philadelphia, many citizens rushed to protect the city. One group was led by two black preachers named Absolom Jones and Richard Allen.

The war finally ended when Great Britain and the United States signed a peace treaty in Belgium late in 1814. One of the people who helped to work out an end to the war was Albert Gallatin, a Pennsylvanian who was active in

Albert Gallatin, a Swiss who settled in Pennsylvania, helped draw up the treaty that ended the War of 1812.

the government in Washington. Because word of the war's end was slow in reaching America, some battles were fought in 1815. The War of 1812 was the last war the Americans ever fought against the British.

CHECKUP

1. What was the Erie Triangle?
2. What made the farmers in western Pennsylvania angry?
3. Who led the American fleet at the battle of Lake Erie?

5/CHAPTER REVIEW

Some Key Terms   On a piece of paper write in the words missing from the sentences below. Use these words: *repeal, patriots, Hessians, Whiskey Rebellion,* and *Constitutional Convention.*

1. The _____ were German soldiers who were hired to fight for the British.

2. The members of the First Continental Congress and others who were against the unfair control of the colonies by Great Britain were known as _____ .

3. The fight of western Pennsylvania farmers against a tax on whiskey was known as the _____ .

4. The colonists wanted King George to _____ , or take back, the new tax laws.

5. At the _____ , representatives from the states met to write a set of laws for the United States.

Do Some Research   Use an encyclopedia or other reference book to find the answers to the following questions.

1. Who was Betsy Ross?

2. Who trained Washington's troops at Valley Forge?

3. What was the Wyoming Massacre?

4. Who were Pennsylvania's representatives at the First Continental Congress?

5. What famous battle of the War of 1812 was fought after the peace treaty ending the war was signed?

For Thought   Write a paragraph or two in answer to one of the following questions.

1. Why, do you think, was Philadelphia made the first capital of the United States of America?

2. Was it fair to give people who had already settled on land in western Pennsylvania first right to buy that land?

KEY FACTS

1. The Algonquians and the Iroquois were two large Indian groups that lived in Pennsylvania.
2. William Penn was made the proprietor, or owner, of the colony of Pennsylvania by the king of England.
3. Quakers and many other groups came to Pennsylvania looking for religious freedom.
4. The Declaration of Independence was passed in Philadelphia on July 4, 1776.
5. The Constitutional Convention was held in Philadelphia.

VOCABULARY QUIZ

Write the numbers 1 through 10 on a piece of paper. Match each word with its definition.

a. maize
b. Lenni-Lenape
c. settler
d. constitution
e. governor
f. bastion
g. ratify
h. representative
i. league
j. flax

1. A person who moves to a new land to live
2. A set of laws by which a place is governed
3. A group of people that joins together for a common purpose
4. Another name for the Delaware Indians
5. Approve
6. A small tower at the point where two walls of a fort meet
7. A plant used to make linen cloth
8. The Indian name for corn
9. The most important leader of a settlement or state
10. Someone people choose to speak for them

REVIEW QUESTIONS

1. Who were the first people in Pennsylvania?
2. Who named the Schuylkill River?
3. When and where did the Swedes first settle in what is now Pennsylvania?
4. What does *Pennsylvania* mean?
5. When did Harrisburg become the capital of Pennsylvania?

ACTIVITIES

1. Draw or make a model of an Algonquian or Iroquois village.
2. Use the card catalog in your library to find a book about one of these topics: Indians, William Penn, the French and Indian War, the Revolutionary War, the War of 1812. Read the book. On a piece of paper, write the title and author of the book and a few sentences telling about the book.
3. Write a skit about one of the following: living on a farm in early Pennsylvania, marching with General Braddock to Fort Duquesne, signing the Declaration of Independence, spending the winter of 1777–1778 at Valley Forge.

FINDING INFORMATION IN A LIBRARY

WHAT IS A CARD CATALOG?

A library is a source of much information. You know that a library has many books. Do you know how to find the one that has the information you need?

One way is by using the card catalog. A card catalog is a listing of all the books in the library. Information about the books is filed on cards that are kept in drawers. Each book is listed alphabetically by the subject, the title, and the author's last name.

In this book you will learn much about Pennsylvania. You may want to find a book that will tell you even more about Pennsylvania. How can you use the card catalog to find such a book?

USING A CARD CATALOG

First, you will look in the card catalog under P for the subject *Pennsylvania*. You will find many cards under this heading. These are subject cards. A subject as broad as Pennsylvania will be broken down further. You will probably see subheadings for cities, climate, geography, government, and so on. These subheadings help narrow the subject. One subheading, *History*, lists a book entitled *Pennsylvania*. The card has a group of numbers or letters that will help you find the book.

You may already know the title of the book you want. Perhaps someone told you that *The Legend of Sleepy Hollow* is a good book about people and goblins. You will look for the title card under the letter *L* for *Legend*. Titles are not alphabetized by *the, a,* or *an.*

A friend of yours may say, "A book by Wallace tells all about ancient Rome, but I have forgotten the title." Then you will look under the letter *W* for *Wallace*. You may find several books by Wallace. These cards are author cards. If you do not know the author's first name, you may have to look through the book titles on the author cards until you find a title that seems to be right. If you find *Ben Hur,* you know that this is probably the book you are looking for.

SKILLS PRACTICE

Now see how well you can use the card catalog. Write down the type of card and the letter under which you will find the following:

a. A book about Harrisburg
b. A book written by Kate Douglas Wiggin
c. A book about Christopher Columbus
d. A book of poems by Riley

You can find information quickly when you know how to use the card catalog. Each time you use the card catalog, it will be easier. If you have questions about the use of the library, the librarian is there to help.

Pennsylvania in the Nineteenth Century

Transportation— The Key to Growth

VOCABULARY

transportation	Allegheny
turnpike	Portage
	Railroad
toll	steamboat
canal	locomotive

Roads   Pennsylvania continued to grow in the 1800s. People moved to all parts of the state. Towns were built and industries were started everywhere. New means of **transportation** were the key to this growth. Transportation is the moving of people and goods from one place to another.

To improve travel between Philadelphia and Lancaster, a new kind of road had been built in the late 1700s. It was called a **turnpike.** At different places on the road, travelers had to pass through a turning gate, or pike, where they paid money called a **toll.** The toll helped to pay for the building costs of the road and its care. The Philadelphia and Lancaster Turnpike Road was the first hard stone road built in America. It was 62 miles (100 km) long. The toll for a wagon at each stop was 4 cents. Soon the Philadelphia and Lancaster Turnpike Road was crowded with stagecoaches and wagons carrying goods and people.

In 1818, another important road opened. It was known as the Cumberland Road or National Road. It ran through southwestern Pennsylvania and was a main road for settlers moving west. By 1840, turnpikes had been built all over Pennsylvania and provided 3,000 miles (4,827 km) of road. Other good roads connected the main cities and towns in the state. The new roads were used by farmers, traders, travelers, and settlers moving west.

Canals   As you learned in Chapter 1, rivers are also used as highways. People in Pennsylvania in the early 1800s soon found that it was cheaper to move goods on the many rivers of the state than on its roads. A boat or barge could carry more goods than many wagons.

Canals in Pennsylvania were used to ship coal from the mines to the factories.

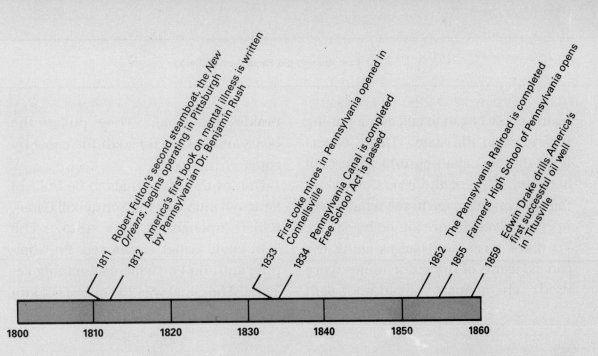

1811   Robert Fulton's second steamboat, the *New Orleans*, begins operating in Pittsburgh

1812   America's first book on mental illness is written by Pennsylvanian Dr. Benjamin Rush

1833   First coke mines in Pennsylvania opened in Connellsville

1834   Pennsylvania Canal is completed Free School Act is passed

1852   The Pennsylvania Railroad is completed

1855   Farmers' High School of Pennsylvania opens

1859   Edwin Drake drills America's first successful oil well in Titusville

| 1800 | 1810 | 1820 | 1830 | 1840 | 1850 | 1860 |

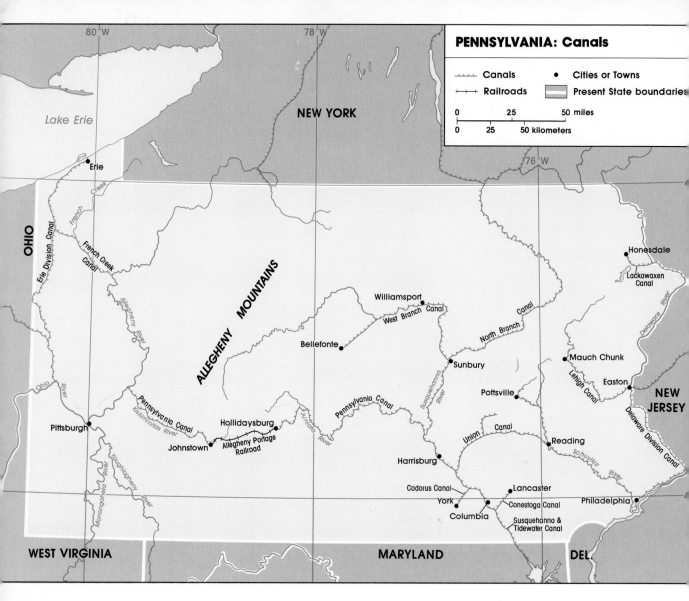

Can you find the Pennsylvania Canal?

Soon people began to talk about joining the rivers in the state. Deep, water-filled ditches called **canals** were built between some of the rivers. Look at the map on this page to see what rivers in Pennsylvania were joined by canals. To move boats and barges along the canals, teams of horses or mules were used. The animals walked on a path beside the canal. They pulled the boats and barges through the canal by rope.

One of the first canals to be built in Pennsylvania was the Schuylkill Canal, which opened in May 1825. The Schuylkill Canal connected Philadelphia and the Pottsville coal-mining region. The canal was 108 miles (174 km) long. Millions of tons of coal were carried on this canal to Philadelphia. Two years later, the Union Canal opened between the Schuylkill and Susquehanna rivers. Other canals followed.

For years, canal builders had dreamed of connecting Philadelphia and Pittsburgh with a canal. In 1834, a canal between the two cities was completed. This canal was known as the Pennsylvania Canal. It started at the town of Columbia, on the Susquehanna River. Goods from Philadelphia were brought to Columbia by railroad. From Columbia the canal ran from the Susquehanna River to the Juniata River. From the Juniata River it went to the town of Hollidaysburg. At Hollidaysburg the canal ran into a problem. There the Allegheny Mountains stood in the way of the canal. To solve this problem, a special railroad was built. The boats and barges were put on railroad cars that horses pulled up the

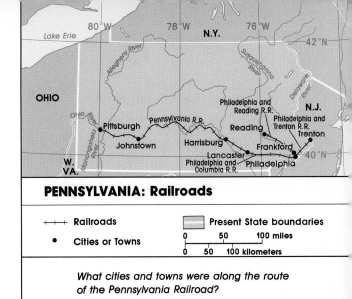

PENNSYLVANIA: Railroads

+—+—+ Railroads

• Cities or Towns

▭ Present State boundaries

0   50   100 miles

0   50   100 kilometers

What cities and towns were along the route of the Pennsylvania Railroad?

mountains. Later, a steam engine was used instead of horses. The steam engine burned coal or wood to heat water. The heated water made steam. The power from the steam made the engine work. It hauled the cars carrying the boats and barges up the mountains. This rail line was called the **Allegheny Portage Railroad.** It was 37 miles (59 km) long. On the other side of the mountains, the boats were put into the water, near Johnstown. From Johnstown the

The Allegheny Portage Railroad helped barges cross the Allegheny Mountains.

canal ran to the Allegheny River, near Pittsburgh. Grain, lumber, coal, iron, and other goods were carried on the Pennsylvania Canal. The canal was a great improvement because it was a cheap way to ship goods from Philadelphia to Pittsburgh.

The steamboat Another change came to the waterways of Pennsylvania during the 1800s. Several people had already tried a new kind of boat called a **steamboat** on the rivers. The boat was not moved by oars or sails but by steam power. By 1787, John Fitch of Philadelphia was running a regular steamboat service across the Delaware River to New Jersey. In 1807, Robert Fulton of Lancaster built a much larger and faster kind of steamboat. The *Clermont,* Fulton's first steamboat, traveled on the Hudson River from New York City to Albany. Fulton's second steamboat, the *New Orleans,* was put into the water at Pittsburgh in 1811. After this, steamboats carried goods from western Pennsylvania down the Ohio and Mississippi rivers. Steamboats were also used on other rivers in the state. Coal, farm products, and manufactured goods were carried faster and more cheaply on steamboats than on other boats. Many of the early steamboats were built at shipyards on the Delaware River.

Railroads The building of canals came to an end in the 1840s. Traffic continued to be heavy on the canals, but railroads slowly took their place.

Horses pulled cars on the first railroads. Then steam power was used. By the 1830s, railroads in Pennsylvania were carrying coal, iron, flour,

Robert Fulton's first steamboat, the Clermont, *was built in 1807.*

The locomotive helped trains move faster. Can you find the locomotive in this painting?

whiskey, and people. The longest railroad in the state was completed in 1852. It ran between Philadelphia and Pittsburgh and was called the Pennsylvania Railroad.

Railroads in Pennsylvania were made better over the years. The first railroad cars did not carry much. Their engines were small and could not pull a heavy load. To produce steam, they burned wood, which gave off a lot of sparks. The first trains also ran on wooden rails, which often split apart. The invention of the iron rail in the early 1800s was a great improvement. In 1860, William Palmer of Philadelphia showed that coal was a better fuel than wood for steam engines. Better **loco-**

motives also began to be built in Pennsylvania at this time. A locomotive is an engine that moves on its own power. Matthias Baldwin of Frankford built many locomotives. His plant in Philadelphia soon made most of the locomotives in America. By the mid-1800s, Pennsylvania led the other states in miles of rail line. There were 2,598 miles (4,180 km) of rail in Pennsylvania by 1860.

CHECKUP

1. What is a turnpike?
2. What was the Allegheny Portage Railroad?
3. What Pennsylvanian built a larger and faster steamboat?
4. What kinds of goods were carried on Pennsylvania's railroads?

Industry and Farming

Coal   Coal was not used much before the 1800s. For heating, people used wood. Wood burned easily and was plentiful. Early in the 1800s, however, coal began to be used as fuel. People found that coal gave off more heat than wood.

Coal mining quickly became a big business in our state. There were large amounts of anthracite northwest of Philadelphia. An anthracite-mining business called the Lehigh Coal Mine Company was the first coal-mining company in the country. Many other mining companies were also started at this time. In 1820, the amount of anthracite mined was only a few thousand tons. As the iron industry and steam engines began to use coal, the amount of anthracite mined jumped to millions of tons.

In western Pennsylvania there was a lot of bituminous coal. When bituminous coal was burned in large ovens, a better kind of fuel was produced. This fuel was called **coke.** When coke

Pennsylvania's forests provided the wood with which early settlers heated their homes.

was used instead of charcoal in an iron furnace, a better kind of iron was produced. In 1833, the first coke ovens opened in Connellsville, just east of Pittsburgh. Soon coke was being used in the iron industry in western Pennsylvania. Coal and coke became the leading goods shipped from western Pennsylvania.

Iron At first the center of the iron industry was in eastern Pennsylvania. For some time the Cornwall iron furnace in Lebanon County was the largest in the state. But as bituminous coal began to be used to make coke, the center of the iron industry moved to the western part of the state. Pittsburgh became known as the Iron City. The Cambria Iron Works in Johnstown opened in 1854 and soon became the largest in the country. By 1860, Pennsylvania was the leading producer of iron in the United States.

Oil Until 1859 all the oil in Pennsylvania was found near the earth's surface. It had worked its way up to the surface from pockets deeper in the earth. Sam Kier of Pittsburgh discovered how to make **kerosene** from oil. Kerosene is a clear liquid that burns easily and gives off bright light. It was a good fuel for lamps. Kerosene lamps were soon found in homes throughout Pennsylvania.

In 1859, America's first oil well was drilled by Edwin Drake in Titusville, Pennsylvania.

In 1859, another Pennsylvanian, Edwin L. Drake, drilled the first successful oil well in the country, at Titusville. Drake's drill struck oil at about 69 feet (21 m). Other people quickly came to the area to drill for oil. A year later, oil wells in the area were producing over 1,000 barrels of oil a day.

Lumber   By the mid-1800s, Pennsylvania was also a leader in the lumber industry.   The industry was centered in the north-central part of the state. Williamsport was the lumber capital of the world for a number of years.

The lumbermen lived in camps in the forests.   Their work was hard.   They cut the trees down, cut off the branches, and sawed the wood into logs. The logs were moved on a special slide to the nearest river, stream, railroad, or road.   At Williamsport and other places the logs were sawed and made into different wood products.

Factories   Other industries grew in Pennsylvania at this time.   Many things, such as wagons, ships and boats, shoes, glass, cement, and **textiles,** were made in factories.   Textiles are woven fabrics or cloth.   The cities of Philadelphia and Pittsburgh became factory centers.   Goods from factories in these cities were shipped on the Delaware, Ohio, Allegheny, and Monongahela rivers.

Workers get together   The workers in the factories and mines of Pennsylvania had three big problems. Their hours were long.   The dangers on the job were great.   Their pay was low.   Many workers spent 12 or more hours a day at work.   Even boys and girls under 12 years of age worked these long hours.   Factories and mines were dangerous places for workers. Many were injured or even killed at work.   Most workers were paid only about $1 a day.

Some workers decided to form groups to make their working conditions better.   The groups they formed

During the 1800s many children worked in Pennsylvania's coal mines.

Pennsylvania's Artists

During the early years of our nation, Philadelphia was our country's center for the arts. The Pennsylvania Academy for the Fine Arts, located in Philadelphia, was the first school of its type in the United States. The academy was founded by the famous American artist, Charles Willson Peale. Peale painted portraits of Benjamin Franklin, George Washington, and many other patriots during the Revolutionary War. Peale's three sons, named Rembrandt, Raphaelle, and Titian after three other famous

painters, were also successful painters.

The most famous artist to paint pictures of life in our new nation was Edward Hicks. Hicks was born into a Quaker family in Bucks County, Pennsylvania.

He liked to paint scenes from the Bible and life on Pennsylvania farms.

Because of these early American artists, we can get an idea of what life in America was like over 200 years ago.

are called **unions.** Craftworkers in Pennsylvania had started unions as early as 1794. But it was not until 1834 that the first national union was formed. In that year, 50 separate unions joined together to form the National Trades Union in Philadelphia.

Many people were against the unions. It was some time before unions were accepted and were able to improve the working conditions and pay of their members. You will read more about unions and workers in Pennsylvania in Chapter 8.

The Smith plow, shown above, was invented in 1800 by Robert and Joseph Smith of Bucks County. The iron-tipped plow allowed farmers to plow their fields more quickly.

Changes in farming The first half of the 1800s was also a time of change in farming in Pennsylvania. Many farmers began to use tools and machines on their farms. Although the new farm machines were still drawn by horses, the work was much easier for the farmer. In 1800, Robert and Joseph Smith of Bucks County invented an iron-tipped plow. With this tool a farmer could plow deeper and more quickly. Some time later, farmers in the state were using new kinds of mowers, rakes, and machines to cut grains and separate their parts. Farmers went to fairs and formed special groups to learn more about the new tools and machines. In 1855, the Farmers' High School of Pennsylvania was formed. This school later became the Agricultural College of Pennsylvania. It is now Pennsylvania State University.

Although industry was growing in Pennsylvania, farming continued to be very important in the state. Pennsylvania was a leading farm state at this time.

CHECKUP

1. What is coke?
2. Who drilled the first successful oil well in the country?
3. Why did workers form unions?
4. What changes came to Pennsylvania farms?

90

Making Life Better

Education   The first schools in Pennsylvania were started by the Quakers. Boys and girls, Quakers and non-Quakers, and whites, blacks, and children of other races went to Quaker schools. Women and men taught in Quaker schools. A Quaker named Olive Songhurst was one of the first women to teach school in America. Other religious groups also ran schools.

Community schools began to open around 1800. It cost money to go to these schools. Poor children could not attend. In 1834, the state government passed the **Free School Act.** Under the Free School Act, schools were free and every child could go to school. Taxes paid for the schools. The Free School Act was the beginning of public schools in Pennsylvania.

Academies also opened at this time. An academy was above an elementary school. Students at an academy learned Greek, Latin, and other subjects. Academy students had to pay for their education. Many towns had their own academies. After studying at an academy, some students went on to college. There were a few colleges in the state before 1800. One of these was the University of Pennsylvania. After 1800, many more colleges opened.

The Friends Meeting House and Academy in Philadelphia was started by the Quakers.

Treatment of the sick   By the middle of the 1800s, there were many good doctors in the state, especially in Philadelphia. There were also hospitals and medical schools in that city. It became an important center of medicine.

One Philadelphia doctor, Benjamin Rush, became well known in America and Europe. Dr. Rush had been a member of the Continental Congress and had signed the Declaration of Independence. He had also served as chief doctor in the Continental army. In 1812, Rush wrote the first book in America on mental illness. It was called *Diseases of the Mind.* His thoughts on how the mentally ill should be helped were very new. He believed that the mentally ill should be treated kindly and gently. At Pennsylvania Hospital in Philadelphia, he was able to follow his beliefs in caring for the mentally ill.

Women's rights   Another area in which progress was made was women's rights. When our nation began, women did not have many rights. They could not vote. They could not hold any public offices. Many women started to believe that they deserved more rights. The fight for women's rights began in Pennsylvania. A Quaker from Philadelphia named Lucretia Mott was a leader in this fight. She often spoke about women's rights.

Dr. Benjamin Rush believed that the mentally ill should be treated gently and kindly.

Lucretia Mott, a Quaker from Philadelphia, was a leader in the women's rights movement.

In 1848, Mott and Elizabeth Cady Stanton held the first women's rights convention in America, at Seneca Falls, New York.

Other Pennsylvanians also worked for the cause of women's rights. Jane Swisshelm of Pittsburgh wrote and gave talks on the subject. Louis Godey of Philadelphia started a women's magazine in 1830. The magazine, known as *Godey's Lady's Book,* had many articles about how women could win their rights. It would be over 75 years before women were given the right to vote, but important steps were being made towards that goal.

CHECKUP

1. When did public schools begin in Pennsylvania?
2. What did Dr. Benjamin Rush do to help the mentally ill?
3. Who spoke out about women's rights in Pennsylvania in the early 1800s?

6/ CHAPTER REVIEW

Some Key Terms On a piece of paper write the words missing from the sentences below. Use these words: *toll, canal, coke, academy, textiles.*

1. An _____ was a school above elementary school, where students learned Greek, Latin, and other subjects.
2. _____ are woven fabrics or cloth.
3. A _____ is a deep, water-filled ditch that connects two waterways.
4. _____ is made by burning bituminous coal in large ovens.
5. Money charged for travel on a turnpike is called a _____ .

Do Some Research Use an encyclopedia or other reference book to find the answers to the following questions.

1. Who invented the steam engine?
2. What was "Old Ironsides"?
3. What colleges and universities in Pennsylvania were founded before 1800?
4. In what year did women in the United States receive the right to vote?

For Thought Write a paragraph or two in answer to one of the following questions.

1. Why did railroads take the place of canals as the most important means of transportation in Pennsylvania?
2. Why did workers in factories and mines form unions?
3. Why was the work that Lucretia Mott and others did for women's rights important?

The Problem of Slavery

> **VOCABULARY**
>
> slavery   plantation
> abolitionist   Underground
>   Railroad

Slaves and free blacks Pennsylvania made great progress in many areas in the early and mid-1800s. In the last chapter you read about some of the ways in which Pennsylvanians tried to make life better in our state. At this same time Pennsylvanians were working hard to make life better for people outside of our state. These Pennsylvanians were working to end **slavery** in the United States. They were called **abolitionists** (ab ə lish' ə nists). Slavery is the practice of one person owning another. A slave is a person who is owned by another person.

Slaves were bought and sold like furniture. They had no rights and had to do whatever their owners said. In early America, black people were brought from Africa and sold as slaves. Owners could buy and sell slaves whenever they wanted. Sometimes families were broken up this way. Most of the slave owners in America lived in the South. They owned large farms there called **plantations** (plan tā' shənz). The plantation owners kept slaves to work in the fields and to do other jobs. The slaves lived in small cabins near the owner's home. They received food and clothing but usually no pay for their work. They were not allowed to learn to read or write.

Not all black people in America were slaves. There were also free blacks in our country. In addition, owners sometimes freed their slaves. Some slaves bought their freedom with money they had saved. Many simply ran away to freedom.

Free blacks worked to help America grow. Blacks had fought in the War for Independence and the War of 1812. Others were doctors, writers, and explorers.

Slaves were used to work in the fields of large plantations in Southern states.

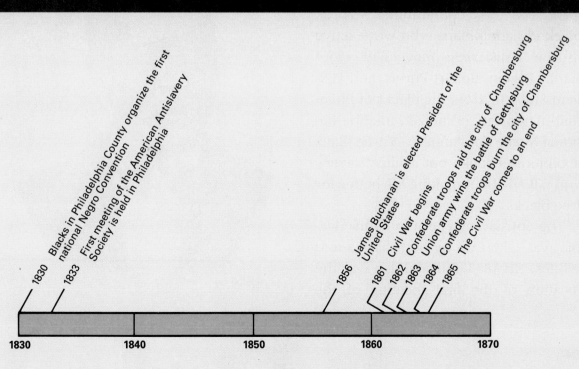

1830 Blacks in Philadelphia County organize the first national Negro Convention

1833 First meeting of the American Antislavery Society is held in Philadelphia

1856 James Buchanan is elected President of the United States

1861 Civil War begins

1862 Confederate troops raid the city of Chambersburg

1863 Union army wins the battle of Gettysburg

1864 Confederate troops burn the city of Chambersburg

1865 The Civil War comes to an end

1830 1840 1850 1860 1870

The slavery question in Pennsylvania   Many in our state were against slavery. Quakers and Mennonites had led a protest against slavery as early as 1688. In the 1750s the Quakers again spoke out against slavery. From that time on, they and other religious groups led the fight to stop the practice. In 1780, Pennsylvania passed the first law in the country to end slavery. It was to do away with slavery over a period of years. The law said that any child born to slaves in the state after 1780 would be a free person when he or she reached the age of 28. By 1800, there was hardly any slavery in Pennsylvania.

There were many free blacks in Pennsylvania in the 1800s. This was especially true in Philadelphia County. In 1830, there were over 10,000 blacks in that county. Many blacks were leaders in their communities. Three black Philadelphians who were active in the antislavery movement were James Forten, Robert Purvis, and William Still. In 1830, the blacks of Philadelphia County organized the first national Negro Convention. Three black abolitionists spoke out against slavery and talked about making life better for free blacks.

The antislavery cause in Pennsylvania was taken up by both blacks and whites. In 1833, Philadelphia was the location of the first meeting of the American Antislavery Society. Robert Purvis became the president of the society. In a few years, meetings of this society were being held in other states. Four years later the Pennsylvania State Antislavery Society gathered for the first time.

Lucretia Mott and her husband, James, were important abolitionists in Pennsylvania. Other Pennsylvania women working to end slavery included Jane Swisshelm, Anne Dickinson, and Ann Preston. Thaddeus Stevens, a representative from Pennsylvania to the United States Congress, also was a leader in the fight to end slavery.

William Still was active in the antislavery movement in Pennsylvania.

The executive committee of the Pennsylvania State Antislavery Society included Lucretia Mott and Robert Purvis (front row, second and third from the right).

These Pennsylvanians and many others gave speeches against slavery. They also organized antislavery groups. Some even helped slaves escape to freedom.

The Underground Railroad

Slaves had been escaping from their owners for years. In the 1830s, however, people began to work together to help slaves escape. These people, both black and white, formed a system to do this. The system was called the **Underground Railroad.** The Underground Railroad was not a railroad with a train and tracks. It was a system of escape paths that slaves could take to freedom. The paths led the slaves from the Southern slave states to free states in the North. The slaves using the Underground Railroad were called passengers. The people who helped slaves on their way were known as conductors. The homes, churches, and other places where slaves hid were known as stations. Pennsylvania was just over the border from Maryland, a slave state. Many slaves first found freedom in Pennsylvania. Columbia, Lancaster, Philadelphia, and Washington, Pennsylvania, were important end points on the railroad.

The most famous conductor on the Underground Railroad was a former slave named Harriet Tubman. She had escaped to freedom from Maryland when she was about 28 years old. In Philadelphia, Tubman met William Still. He was an important member of the Underground Railroad and later wrote a history of the system. With Still's help, Tubman went back to the South many times. She led hundreds of people to freedom over the years. Her work as a conductor was so well-known that slave owners offered rewards totaling $40,000 for her capture.

The painting below shows how Henry Clay, a slave from Richmond, Virginia, escaped to Philadelphia in a crate.

Harriet Tubman, a former slave, was the most famous conductor of the Underground Railroad.

Many slaves escaped from Maryland, a slave state, to freedom in Pennsylvania.

In 1850, the United States Congress passed the Fugitive Slave Law. Under the law it was a crime to help a runaway slave. This law made work on the Underground Railroad as dangerous in the North as it was in the South. Many Pennsylvanians hid slaves in their homes. Robert Purvis had a secret room in his home in Philadelphia where he hid runaway slaves. The room could be reached only through a trap door. Because of the Fugitive Slave Law, after many slaves were helped to the North, they were led into Canada for their own safety. In 1852, William Still and other Philadelphians reorganized the Vigilant Committee. The committee had been started earlier by Purvis to help runaway slaves. The new committee paid for runaway slaves' needs while they were in Philadelphia. It also paid for the slaves' trips to Canada.

More and more people in the North joined the antislavery movement and helped slaves to freedom. By 1860, the Underground Railroad had helped over 50,000 slaves to escape to the North. But the Underground Railroad was not a real answer to the problem of slavery. Differences between the North and the South over slavery were greater than ever before.

CHECKUP

1. What is an abolitionist?
2. Who was Harriet Tubman?
3. How did the Fugitive Slave Law affect the workings of the Underground Railroad?

99

The President from Pennsylvania

Buchanan's early life   It was during this troubled time in our nation's history that the only President from Pennsylvania was elected. His name was James Buchanan. Buchanan was born on April 23, 1791, in a log cabin at Stony Batter in Franklin County. His father, who was from Ireland, had set up a trading post there, on the road from Philadelphia to Pittsburgh. Later the Buchanans moved to Mercersburg, where James studied at the Old Stone Academy. He also helped in his father's store in the town. In 1807, Buchanan began his studies at Dickinson College in Carlisle. He was one of only 42 students at the college.

Law and politics   After his graduation from Dickinson in 1809, Buchanan began to study law in Lancaster, which was the state capital at the time. This could be said to be the beginning of his career in **politics.** Politics is the art or science of guiding government. When Buchanan became a lawyer in 1812, he also became active in local politics. From 1814 to 1816 he was involved in state politics in Harrisburg. Four years later he was elected as representative from Dauphin, Lebanon, and Lancaster counties to the United States Congress.

James Buchanan was born in this log cabin at Stony Batter, Pennsylvania.

James Buchanan was the only President of the United States to come from Pennsylvania. He was elected as our fifteenth President in 1856.

In Washington, D.C., Buchanan soon became a member of the Democratic party. He served as a representative from 1820 to 1830. In 1831, President Andrew Jackson asked Buchanan to be America's representative in Russia. Buchanan helped to settle the first trade treaty between the United States and Russia. When Buchanan returned from Russia, he went to Washington again. He served in the United States Congress for 11 more years. In the government in Washington, Buchanan spoke out on the slavery question. Although he was against slavery, he believed that laws could not change people's views of slavery. He tried without great success to make others understand this and stop arguing about slavery.

When James Polk became President in 1845, he asked Buchanan to work under him. During Polk's Presidency, our country grew in size. Buchanan took steps to make Texas a state. But Mexico claimed Texas and became angry at this idea. It was only after a war with Mexico that Texas became a state. Buchanan also helped to set the boundaries of a **territory** in the northwestern United States known as Oregon Country. A territory is an area of land.

In 1849, Buchanan left Washington and politics for Pennsylvania and a private life. He bought Wheatland, a large, beautiful home in Lancaster, and spent his time gardening and working on his new house.

Buchanan as President   While serving as minister to England under President Franklin Pierce, Buchanan got a chance to run for President. In 1856 he was the Democratic **candidate** for President. A candidate is a person chosen by a group to run for an office. The Democrats' message to the people of the country was that it was important to keep the Northern and Southern

101

states together as the United States of America. Buchanan won the election. The issue of slavery was very important in the election and continued to be important in Buchanan's presidency.

As President, Buchanan tried to bring Northerners and Southerners together by asking both to serve in different offices under him. But many believed that he liked the South better. This may have been because Buchanan still held that it was a person's choice whether to have slaves or not. States and territories, he believed, should make this decision for themselves. In 1857, when Kansas was about to become a state, some settlers in the territory wrote a constitution that would make Kansas a slave state. President Buchanan supported the people's right to make this choice. He urged Congress to accept the constitution. But Congress refused and sent it back to Kansas. Antislavery settlers in the territory voted it down. When Kansas became a state 4 years later, it was a free state.

Many people were angry about the President's action in the case of Kansas. Many more people than before believed that he favored the South. In 1858, more Northerners, many of them members of the Republican party, were elected to Congress.

They made it difficult for Buchanan to do the things he wanted to do as President. The slavery question was also beginning to divide members of the Democratic party. Buchanan was not chosen again as the Democratic candidate for President. In 1860, a Republican was elected President. His name was Abraham Lincoln.

Before Lincoln became President in March 1861, Buchanan was faced with great problems. Some of the states in the South wanted to form a new country. In December 1860, South Carolina **seceded,** or withdrew, from the United States of America. Six other states joined South Carolina in February 1861 to form the Confederate States of America. President Buchanan said

Because of fighting between proslavery and antislavery groups, Kansas became known as "Bleeding Kansas."

Wheatland, located in Lancaster, was the home of James Buchanan.

that these states did not have the right to do this. But he also said that the United States Constitution did not tell how to stop the seven states from doing what they wanted to do. He suggested that the Constitution be changed to allow for the views of both free and slave states. Others were against this idea.

It was Buchanan's greatest hope that war would not break out between North and South. Although no blood was shed during his time as President, shots were fired in South Carolina. South Carolina had asked Buchanan to make United States troops leave Fort Sumter in Charleston, South Carolina. But he refused to surrender the fort. When a ship was sent to the fort with fresh troops, soldiers from South Carolina fired on the ship.

When Buchanan left office, the country was still at peace. He spent the rest of his life at Wheatland. He died there on June 1, 1868.

CHECKUP
1. Where and when was James Buchanan born?
2. What was Buchanan's view of slavery?
3. Why did some people believe that President Buchanan favored the South?

The Civil War

War begins   War began on April 12, 1861, at Fort Sumter. Southern soldiers again attacked the fort. The soldiers in the fort were forced to surrender. News of this attack shocked many Americans. Northerners rushed to fight for the **Union.** The Union was another name for the states that did not secede from the United States. Four more slave states joined the Confederate States of America; the other four stayed in the Union. The map on page 105 shows how the country was divided. The war was called the **Civil War.** A civil war is a war between people of the same country.

Pennsylvania plays an important role   Pennsylvania was important to the Union from the start of the war. It

The attack on Fort Sumter by Southern soldiers was the beginning of the Civil War.

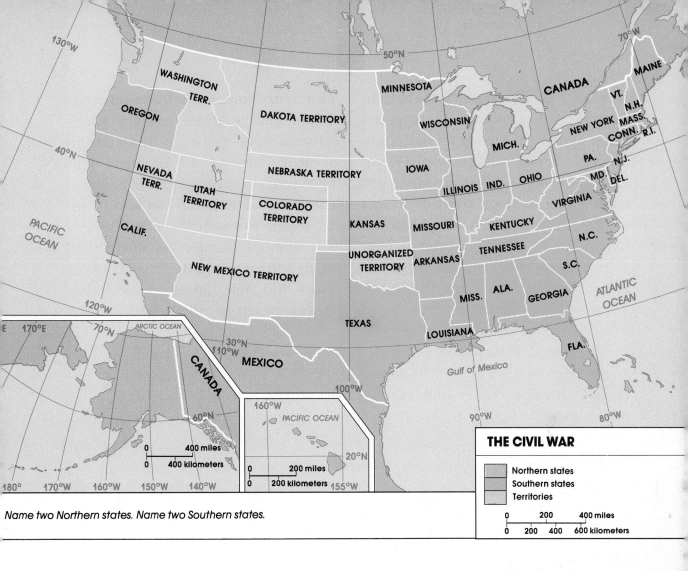

THE CIVIL WAR

| Northern states |
| Southern states |
| Territories |

0   200   400 miles
0   200   400   600 kilometers

Name two Northern states. Name two Southern states.

was the first state to raise troops to fight for the North. President Lincoln asked for 14 regiments from the state. Pennsylvania answered with 25 regiments. Six days after the war started, 530 soldiers from Pennsylvania rushed to Washington, D.C., to guard the capital. During the war nearly 350,000 soldiers and 14,000 sailors from our state served in the Union army and navy. Factories in Pennsylvania made uniforms for the troops. Rifles, cannons, and shells were made in Pittsburgh and Philadelphia. Ships were built in our state. Railroads in Pennsylvania carried troops and goods needed by the army.

Jay Cooke, a banker in Philadelphia, raised money for the Union. Simon Cameron and Thomas Scott, both Pennsylvanians, served under President Lincoln in the Department of War. The governor of Pennsylvania, Andrew G. Curtin, was a strong supporter of the President and often advised him.

Pennsylvania became a place to train soldiers for the Union army. A special camp opened in Montgomery County in 1863. It was called Camp William Penn. During the war, about 11,000 black soldiers were trained at this camp. They went on to fight in the Union army. Camp Curtin, named after the governor, was an important Union troop center at Harrisburg. A number of army and navy leaders were from Pennsylvania, including Generals George B. McClellan, George G. Meade, and Winfield S. Hancock; and Admiral David D. Porter and Rear Admiral John A. Dahlgren.

The war comes to Pennsylvania
Confederate soldiers invaded Pennsylvania three times. In the autumn of 1862, General J.E.B. Stuart and 1,800 soldiers reached Chambersburg. They circled General McClellan and his troops to reach the town, which was a supply center for the Union. Stuart and his troops destroyed a storehouse and stole horses and supplies. Then they left as quickly as they had come. They completely escaped the notice of McClellan and his men.

Stuart's raid on Chambersburg surprised and scared Pennsylvania. The Confederate army had an easy road

Many of the blacks who fought for the Union were trained at Camp William Penn.

The Confederate soldiers captured Carlisle and got very close to Harrisburg. Union soldiers led by General George Meade met the Confederate soldiers at the town of Gettysburg. One third of Meade's army was made up of soldiers from Pennsylvania. From July 1 to July 3 the fighting raged. Thousands of soldiers on both sides were killed or wounded. Finally, Lee and his men had to retreat. The North had won the battle of Gettysburg.

General George B. McClellan, from Pennsylvania, was a leader of the Union army during the Civil War.

Pennsylvanians from throughout our state helped in many ways during the Civil War. Here forts are being built to protect the Union army from an attack by the army of General Robert E. Lee.

into Pennsylvania through the Cumberland Valley. Soldiers could march or ride up the Great Valley from Virginia to Pennsylvania. In June 1863, General Robert E. Lee led a major invasion of 75,000 men into Pennsylvania. Lee hoped to attack the center of the state and destroy the war industries and Union transportation center there. Without supplies, bridges, and railroads the Union would not be able to move.

The battle of Gettysburg was fought from July 1 to July 3, 1863. Thousands of soldiers from both sides died during the battle. This battle was the turning point of the Civil War. Four months later, President Lincoln gave his famous Gettysburg Address at the site of the battle.

The battle of Gettysburg has become the most famous battle of the Civil War. It is also considered to be the turning point of the war. Four months later, President Lincoln made a special trip to Gettysburg to dedicate a cemetery on the battlefield. He also made a speech that became very famous. It is called the Gettysburg Address.

Southern troops entered Pennsylvania a third time, in July 1864. They went again to the town of Chambersburg. They told the people of Chambersburg that they would burn the town unless they were paid a large sum of money. The people of the town refused to pay, so the Confederate soldiers burned the town. Most of the people in Chambersburg were left without homes. Almost $2 million worth of damage was done. The Civil War continued for almost one year after the burning of Chambersburg.

The war comes to an end   The North finally won the war in 1865. The end of the Civil War brought two important results. First, all the states were part of the Union again. Second, slavery was ended in the United States. Pennsylvanians could be proud that they helped to win the war.

CHECKUP

1. How did Pennsylvania help the Union during the Civil War?
2. Who was governor of our state during the war?
3. What battle was the turning point of the war?

7/CHAPTER REVIEW

Some Key Terms   On a piece of paper write the words missing from the sentences below. Use these words: *slavery, territory, secede, Civil War, Union.*

1. South Carolina was the first state to _____, or withdraw, from the Union.
2. The practice of one person owning another is _____.
3. A _____ is an area of land.
4. The _____ was a war between the people of our country.
5. The _____ is another name for the states that did not join the Confederate States of America.

Do Some Research   Use an encyclopedia or other reference book to find the answers to the following questions.

1. What were the main paths of the Underground Railroad?
2. What was the Dred Scott case?
3. Why is the battle of Gettysburg known as the turning point of the Civil War?
4. How many soldiers died in the Civil War?

For Thought   Write a paragraph or two in answer to one of the following questions.
1. Why, do you think, did some people risk everything to help slaves gain their freedom?
2. Do you agree with James Buchanan's views on slavery? Why?
3. Why was Pennsylvania so important to the Union during the Civil War?

Pennsylvania Becomes an Industrial Giant

VOCABULARY

brittle
steel
Bessemer process

open-hearth process
strike
five-and-dime store

The steel industry   Pennsylvania's industries had helped the nation greatly during the Civil War. After the war, industry in our state grew as never before. By 1900, Pennsylvania was a leading industrial state.

As you know, Pennsylvania had been a leader in the iron industry since the 1700s. Iron is a hard metal, but it is **brittle.** This means that it breaks easily. A stronger iron product was needed. This product was **steel.** In the 1850s, two men discovered a new way to make steel. One of these men was Henry Bessemer (bes' ə mər), of England; the other was William Kelly, of Pittsburgh. They both designed a special furnace container called a converter for making steel. Melted iron was poured into the converter. Then cold air was blown through the melted iron through pipes in the bottom of the converter. This burned out the impurities, or bad parts, in the iron and changed them into a gas. The gas then caught on fire. This heated the iron even more and produced steel. Because some people believed that Bessemer was the one who discovered this way of making steel, it is called the **Bessemer process.**

This process was first used successfully in Pennsylvania at the Cambria Iron Works in Johnstown in 1861-1862. But only after the Civil War was steel made in large quantities. The Bessemer process was also used in the 1870s by the Pennsylvania Steel Company, at Steelton, and the Freedom Iron and Steel Works, at Lewistown.

Pittsburgh quickly became the steelmaking center of the nation. A new source of iron ore had been found in the Lake Superior region. Iron ore

Shown on the opposite page is the Jones and Laughlin Iron Works in Pittsburgh. After the Civil War, Pittsburgh became the steelmaking center of the United States.

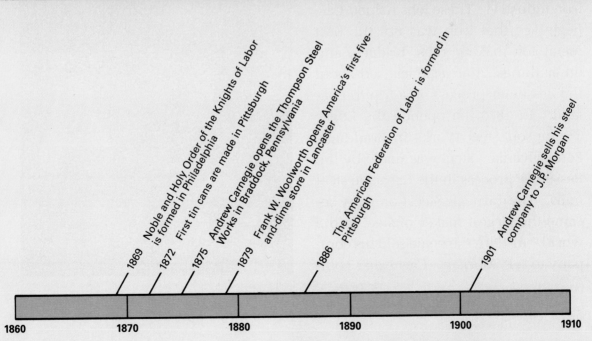

1869 Noble and Holy Order of the Knights of Labor is formed in Philadelphia

1872 First tin cans are made in Pittsburgh

1875 Andrew Carnegie opens the Thompson Steel Works in Braddock, Pennsylvania

1879 Frank W. Woolworth opens America's first five-and-dime store in Lancaster

1886 The American Federation of Labor is formed in Pittsburgh

1901 Andrew Carnegie sells his steel company to J.P. Morgan

| 1860 | 1870 | 1880 | 1890 | 1900 | 1910 |

could be shipped across the Great Lakes and then brought by rail to Pittsburgh. Pittsburgh was in the middle of the bituminous coal region of Pennsylvania, which supplied coke as a fuel for the furnaces. There were also business people in Pittsburgh to lead the way in steelmaking. One of these people was Andrew Carnegie.

Andrew Carnegie was born in Scotland in 1835. His family came to the United States when he was a boy. They settled in Allegheny City, which is now part of Pittsburgh. At the age of 13, Carnegie got his first job, as a worker in a cotton mill. Over the next few years he moved from one job to another. Each new job was better than the one before.

Before and during the Civil War, Carnegie worked for the Pennsylvania Railroad. After the war he entered the iron industry. These jobs helped Carnegie see that iron was not the best metal for making rails, bridges, and other things. Carnegie learned about the Bessemer process on a trip to England. In 1875, he opened the Edgar Thompson Steel Works in Braddock, Pennsylvania. Steel was made by the Bessemer process in the Carnegie steel mills. The Carnegie Steel Company became the largest maker of steel in the world. In 1901, Carnegie sold his company to J. P. Morgan. Carnegie's company was put together with other steel companies to form the United States Steel Corporation. Carnegie had made millions of dollars in steelmaking. He gave millions to build libraries, museums, and concert halls. He believed that some of his fortune should be used for the good of the people.

Andrew Carnegie used his money to help others by building museums, libraries, and concert halls.

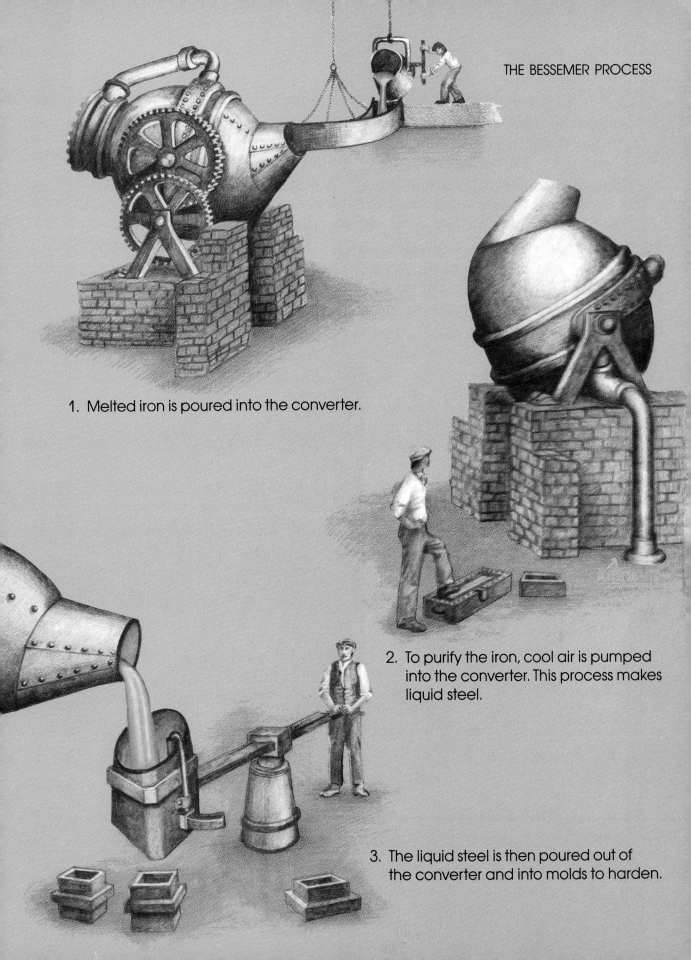

THE BESSEMER PROCESS

1. Melted iron is poured into the converter.

2. To purify the iron, cool air is pumped into the converter. This process makes liquid steel.

3. The liquid steel is then poured out of the converter and into molds to harden.

Toward the end of the 1800s, the **open-hearth process** was being used in a large number of steel mills. In the open-hearth process, a bowl-shaped furnace was used to heat iron. The iron could be heated to higher temperatures in this type of furnace. Samples could be taken from the furnace and tested for quality. Although it took longer to make steel this way, a better kind of steel was produced. By 1908 more open-hearth steel was made than Bessemer steel.

Coal becomes king   After the Civil War there was a greater need for coal. New railroads and the new steel industry needed more coal. The amount of coal mined in Pennsylvania jumped from about 15 million tons (14 million t) in 1860 to 100 million tons (91 million t) after the war. Almost twice as much anthracite was mined as bituminous coal until 1890. By 1900, more bituminous coal was mined than anthracite.

The steel mills needed ·most of the

The Thompson Steel Works was opened by Andrew Carnegie in Braddock, Pennsylvania, in 1875. The Bessemer process was used at this steel mill.

bituminous coal for coke. Coke was made by heating soft coal. It was used for heating furnaces to make steel. New kinds of ovens made better coke more quickly than before. These ovens also captured gases given off by the coal as it turned into coke. The gases could be used to make materials such as fuels, fertilizer, and cleaning fluid. The person who owned most of the new coke ovens was Henry C. Frick, of Fayette County. Frick had more coke ovens than anyone else in America. In the 1880s, Frick became an important partner in the Carnegie Steel Company.

Coal was the leading mineral mined in Pennsylvania in the late 1800s. It earned millions of dollars for our state. Coal mining gave work to thousands of people.

Unions To improve their working conditions and pay, workers again formed unions, as they had in the early 1800s. Groups of workers from the

Coke was made by heating soft coal in very hot furnaces. Coke was used for melting down iron ore, which was important to Pennsylvania's steel industry.

The United Mine Workers of America fought for better wages and better working conditions for coal miners.

American Federation of Labor. The American Federation of Labor was started in Pittsburgh in 1886. It brought together many smaller unions from different industries.

Striking was one way that unions tried to make working conditions and pay better. When workers **strike,** they stop working. When a company did not give its workers what they thought was fair, the workers went on strike. Some strikes were violent. However, many strikes did make gains for the workers and their unions.

In 1892 a strike took place at the Carnegie Steel Company plant in Homestead, Pennsylvania. During this strike, known as the Homestead Strike, violence broke out and state troops had to restore order.

coal, iron and steel, and railroad industries formed large unions. Soon workers began to think about forming a national union that would have members from many industries. In 1869, the Noble and Holy Order of the Knights of Labor was formed in Philadelphia. Its members were from different industries. They may have numbered over 700,000 at one point. The Knights of Labor wanted an 8-hour workday, and laws for health and safety and against child labor. Later the Knights were replaced by the

Cities grow As industry grew, so did the cities of Pennsylvania. The growing industries of Pennsylvania needed a lot of workers. To find them, mills and factories were built in and near cities. Other cities grew because of industry nearby. By 1900, about 80 percent of the workers in manufacturing in Pennsylvania lived in cities.

The city of Altoona grew because of the railroad-car manufacturing business there. Scranton, Wilkes-Barre, Hazleton, and Pottsville grew with the coal industry. Oil City sprang up with the oil industry in the area. Williamsport continued to grow with the lumber industry. Many kinds of industry helped the cities of Philadelphia and Pittsburgh grow.

New needs arose with the larger numbers of people living in the cities. Food presented a major problem. In 1872, the first tin cans were made in Pittsburgh. Food in tin cans stayed fresh for a long time. Henry J. Heinz, of Pittsburgh, started a food-processing plant in that city. The plant provided food in jars and cans. Now people in the cities could have fresh food without going to the country to buy it or growing it themselves.

Buying clothes and household items was also a problem for people in the cities. Many worked long hours for little pay. They did not have time to look for what they needed at many different

By the end of the 1800s, Pennsylvania was a leading industrial state.

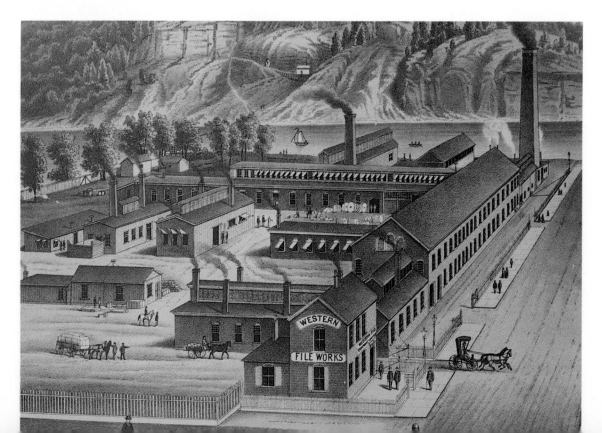

The F. & J. Heinz Company has become famous for its jarred pickles. Today, Heinz produces many other kinds of foods. Can you name any?

stores. John Wanamaker answered the needs of the people of Philadelphia by opening a department store in 1876. It was the first department store in America. All kinds of things were sold there. People saved time by shopping at Wanamaker's. In 1879, Frank W. Woolworth opened a store in Lancaster. Things did not cost much at this new store. Items were sold for 5 and 10 cents. When Woolworth died in 1919, there were over 1,000 of his stores in America. They were known as **five-and-dime stores.**

At Frank W. Woolworth's five-and-dime stores, items sold for 5 and 10 cents.

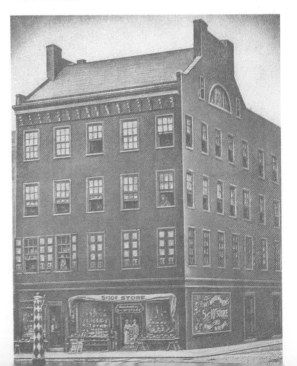

George Westinghouse

Pennsylvania has been the home of many great inventors. One was George Westinghouse. As a boy, Westinghouse worked in his father's machine shop. At the age of 15, he invented a new kind of engine. It was called a rotary engine. Westinghouse never patented this idea. He left his father's machine shop to fight for the Union during the Civil War.

After the war, Westinghouse discovered a way to get trains to stop more quickly and safely. He invented a brake that worked on air pressure. By 1872, his air brake was being used all over the world. He organized the Westinghouse Air Brake Company in Pittsburgh to make this new invention.

Over the years, Westinghouse worked on many other inventions. These included a new safety signal for railroads and the first diesel train locomotive to run on oil. Altogether, Westinghouse took out over 400 patents.

The work of George Westinghouse has helped to make our country great. In 1955 he was elected to the American Hall of Fame. All Americans can be proud of this great inventor.

Other problems in the cities were not solved right away. Housing was a problem, although the streets of cities such as Philadelphia were crowded with houses. Some companies owned houses for their workers. But very often these houses were not kept up. Fresh, pure water was hard to get in some cities, such as Pittsburgh. Still, the cities continued to grow as more and more people came to the cities to work and live.

CHECKUP

1. Who helped the steel industry grow in Pittsburgh?
2. What was the leading mineral mined in Pennsylvania in the late 1800s?
3. What did John Wanamaker and Frank W. Woolworth do to help people in the cities?

New People Arrive

Immigrants come to Pennsylvania   When the new mills, mines, and factories opened in the late 1800s, there were not enough workers in our state to do the work. Workers had to be found somewhere else. At this time millions of people began to come to live and work in the United States from other countries. People who leave their homes in one country and move to another country to live are called **immigrants** (im′ ə grənts).

These immigrants to Pennsylvania are crossing the Appalachian Mountains to get to their new home.

More immigrants came to Pennsylvania than to any other state except New York. Before the Civil War many people from Ireland, Wales, England, and Scotland had come to Pennsylvania. They found jobs building canals and railroads and mining coal. Some farmed. After the Civil War more Irish immigrants came to our state. They were joined by a large number of Germans. Some of the Germans settled on farms. Many Germans and Irish settled in cities and worked in the coal and iron and steel industries. By 1890, the Irish were the largest group of immigrants in the state.

From the 1880s on, a new group of people began to arrive in Pennsylvania. They were immigrants from southern and eastern Europe. People from Italy, Poland, and Russia came in the largest numbers. Other European immigrants came from the countries now known as Hungary, Yugoslavia, Lithuania, and Czechoslovakia. Again, the newcomers went to the cities and mining regions and took jobs in the coal and iron and steel industries.

Problems faced by the newcomers   Suppose your family left the United States and moved to another country to live. What do you think your new life would be like? What problems would you face? What if you

Pennsylvania became the new home for immigrants from many European countries.

did not speak the language that was spoken in your new country? How would you learn about the laws and customs there? Could you find a job? The immigrants who came to Pennsylvania faced these problems.

Most of the immigrants had lived and worked on farms in Europe. But when they arrived in Pennsylvania, most had to live in cities and find work in mills, factories, or mines. Many lived in crowded buildings near their place of work. For many of the immigrants, English was a strange language.

Immigrants from one country often lived together in one neighborhood. There they could continue to speak their own language and live the way they had in their old country. A neighborhood in which people from the

same country or of the same background live together is called an **ethnic neighborhood.** Today many cities of Pennsylvania still have ethnic neighborhoods where immigrants of the 1800s and early 1900s settled. Usually these neighborhoods have stores and businesses much like those in the immigrants' old country. Places of worship are also important parts of ethnic neighborhoods.

Many immigrant groups found their churches and other places of worship were a great help in getting settled and feeling at home in their new country. Classes and programs were set up by churches and other religious organizations for immigrant children and their parents. The state also held classes to teach the immigrants English and to help them become American citizens. Many of the children of the immigrants have become leaders in their communities and in our country.

The heritage of Pennsylvanians
In your community there are many clues to people's backgrounds and **heritage.** Heritage is the customs and beliefs handed down from one generation to the next. Look at place-names, places of worship, and shops and other businesses in your community. Where did the Pennsylvanians in your community come from? Where did

Many people from countries all over the world become United States citizens every year.

your own family come from? Why did your family and others come to live in Pennsylvania? What customs and beliefs did they bring? Be proud of your background and heritage. Learn to appreciate the background and heritage of others.

CHECKUP

1. What is an immigrant?
2. What three groups from southern and eastern Europe came to Pennsylvania in the largest numbers?
3. How did living in a neighborhood together help immigrants from one country?

8/ CHAPTER REVIEW

Some Key Terms On a piece of paper write the words missing from the sentences below. Use these words: *steel, Bessemer process, strike, heritage, immigrants.*

1. When workers _____, they stop working.

2. People who leave their homes in one country and move to another country to live are called _____.

3. The _____ was a new way to make steel.

4. _____ is a strong iron product that does not break easily.

5. Customs and beliefs handed down from one generation to the next are a people's _____.

Do Some Research Use an encyclopedia or other reference book to find the answers to the following questions.

1. How much steel is made in Pennsylvania today?

2. What was the result of the Homestead Strike?

3. Name some of the ethnic neighborhoods in Pennsylvania cities today.

For Thought Write a paragraph or two in answer to one of the following questions.

1. Did the workers in the 1890s need labor unions?

2. Why does a state need a large population to become an important manufacturing center?

KEY FACTS

1. Pennsylvania led the nation in building turnpikes, canals, and railroads.

2. Pennsylvania made great progress in education, medicine, and women's rights in the early 1800s.

3. James Buchanan, the fifteenth President of the United States, was from Pennsylvania.

4. The battle of Gettysburg was the turning point of the Civil War.

5. Andrew Carnegie helped steelmaking become an important industry in our state.

6. Immigrants from Europe came to our state in large numbers in the late 1800s.

VOCABULARY QUIZ

Write the numbers 1 through 10 on a piece of paper. Match each term with its definition.

a. turnpike
b. union
c. Free School Act
d. abolitionist
e. Underground Railroad
f. candidate
g. politics
h. brittle
i. ethnic neighborhood
j. plantation

1. The art or science of guiding government

2. A group formed by workers to make their working conditions better

3. A person chosen by a group to run for an office

4. A person who worked to end slavery

5. A road on which travelers pass through a turning gate where they pay a toll

6. A large farm in the South

7. A law under which schools were free and every child could go to school

8. A system of escape paths that slaves could take to freedom

9. Breaking easily

10. A neighborhood in which people from the same country live together

REVIEW QUESTIONS

1. What Pennsylvanian built a larger and faster steamboat?

2. Why was William Still important in the years before the Civil War?

3. How did Pennsylvania help the Union in the Civil War?

4. What problems did immigrants face?

ACTIVITIES

1. Use an encyclopedia or other reference book to look up information about one of the following: canals, steamboats, railroads, coal mining, lumbering, steelmaking. Write a two-paragraph essay about the topic you chose.

2. Interview your grandparents or an older family friend to learn something about your family's heritage. Write what you learn in a paragraph describing your family's background.

USING A DICTIONARY

WHAT IS A DICTIONARY?

A dictionary is a book that contains the words of a language. A dictionary tells several things about these words. The pronunciation and the meaning of each word is given. The respelling shows you how to pronounce or say a word. It divides the word into parts and identifies the sounds of the letters.

The words are listed in alphabetical order. This helps you find the words easily. It also makes it possible for you to easily check the spelling of a word.

When you see a word that you do not know, you can find the meaning of the word in a dictionary. If you do not know how to use a word, a dictionary can help.

Look up the word *transportation* in a dictionary. Why is it easy to find? (Words are in alphabetical order.) Notice that the word is divided into parts. Look at the respelling. Use the respelling to help you say the word. How many definitions are given for the word *transportation?*

SKILLS PRACTICE

Look up the following words in a dictionary. Write a sentence, using each word.

1. canal
2. toll
3. union
4. textile
5. plantation
6. slavery
7. candidate
8. territory
9. academy
10. steel
11. strike
12. heritage
13. immigrant
14. brittle

Some students say, "If I can't spell a word, how can I look it up in the dictionary?" Usually you can spell a word close enough to search and find it in the dictionary. Use a dictionary to correct these misspelled words. The misspelled part is underlined. Write the correct spellings on a piece of paper.

1. pracess
2. poeple
3. futire
4. countrys
5. locamotive
6. kerocene
7. railrood
8. abolision
9. cesede
10. cival

Pennsylvania Today

From 1900 to the end of World War I

┌─ VOCABULARY ─────────────
│ wage   alliance
│ Workmen's   armistice
│   Compensation
│   Act
└──────────────────────────

Pennsylvania's population grows
The years between 1900 and 1920 were a time of great population growth in Pennsylvania. Between 1900 and 1910, the number of people in the state increased from about 6 million to 8 million. Most of the new people were immigrants. Thousands of them found work in the United States Steel Corporation. U.S. Steel had hundreds of mills and coal and limestone mines in Pennsylvania. The hard work of new people in our state helped make the United States Steel Corporation the largest producer of steel in America. Other immigrants found work in other industries in our state.

Changes in labor and industry
Everything did not go well for the workers in our state. The work was still as long, hard, and dangerous as it had been in the 1800s. The coal mines were especially bad. Each year, hundreds of workers were killed or injured in accidents in the mines. Even though their work was very dangerous, the miners were paid a low **wage.** A wage is a payment of money for services.

In 1902, the miners in the anthracite mines in eastern Pennsylvania went on strike. They were led by John A. Mitchell, the president of a union formed in 1890 called the United Mine Workers of America. The miners wanted safer working conditions and higher wages. The strike lasted for many months. As the winter months drew near, President Theodore Roosevelt feared that people would not have enough coal to heat their homes. President Roosevelt got the mine owners and the miners' union to talk together. The owners gave the miners a 10 percent raise in pay. They also shortened the workday from over 10 hours to 9 hours. These were real improvements for the miners.

The Pennsylvania coal strike of 1902 was finally settled after President Theodore Roosevelt (in the white coat) met with the miners' union and the mine owners.

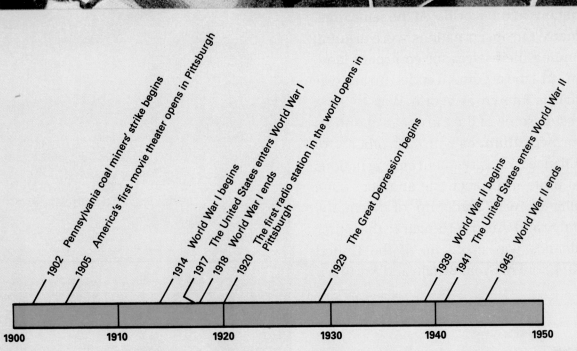

Pennsylvania coal miners' strike begins

America's first movie theater opens in Pittsburgh

World War I begins

The United States enters World War I

World War I ends

The first radio station in the world opens in Pittsburgh

The Great Depression begins

World War II begins

The United States enters World War II

World War II ends

1902 1905   1914 1917 1918 1920   1929   1939 1941 1945

1900   1910   1920   1930   1940   1950

The Pennsylvania government also helped to improve the working conditions in factories and mines. In 1913 a new state office was set up. It was called the Department of Labor and Industry. This department's job was to protect workers from unsafe working conditions. It passed safety rules and inspected factories and mines to make sure that the rules were followed. The state government also set up a special fund to pay injured workers. To get money for this, a law called the **Workmen's Compensation Act** was passed in 1915. The Workmen's Compensation Act made owners of industries pay some of the medical bills of workers injured on the job.

World War I   The industries in Pennsylvania were helping the United States grow into one of the strongest nations in the world. At the same time, many European nations were arguing among themselves for control of land. In 1914 the argument ended up in a war that is known as World War I. As a result, some of the European countries formed **alliances** with each other. An alliance is an agreement among nations to unite to protect one another. One alliance was made up of Germany, Italy, and Austria-Hungary; the other alliance was made up of the United Kingdom of Great Britain and Northern

Ireland, France, and Russia. In 1917 the United States joined the United Kingdom, France, and Russia.

As in past wars, Pennsylvania helped to support the war effort. Ships for the navy were built in Philadelphia and Chester. The steel mills of Pittsburgh and factories across the state made weapons for the army. About 300,000 Pennsylvanians served in the army and navy during World War I. Two people from our state were leaders in the military. Tasker H. Bliss was the commanding officer of the army, and William S. Sims commanded the navy.

Tasker H. Bliss (on right) was the commanding officer of the United States Army during World War I.

To celebrate Armistice Day, many cities held parades. These men are watching the 1919 Armistice Day parade on Broad Street in Philadelphia.

World War I ended when Germany surrendered on November 11, 1918. Germany asked for an **armistice.** An armistice is an agreement between countries to stop fighting each other. In honor of all those who died in the war, November 11 was made a holiday in the United States. This holiday was called Armistice Day. In 1954, President Dwight D. Eisenhower made November 11 Veterans Day in honor of all those who fought in any of America's wars. We still celebrate Veterans Day today.

CHECKUP

1. Who helped end the coal miners' strike of 1902?
2. Whose side did America join in World War I?
3. How did Pennsylvania help the war effort during World War I?

The 1920s and the Great Depression

VOCABULARY

leisure time   depression
pollute   rural
economy

Changes in the 1920s   As the 1920s began, the Pennsylvania steel mills and coal mines that helped to supply American forces during World War I continued to grow. The new automobile industry needed more steel. Most of it came from Pennsylvania mills. This meant that more coal was needed for the steel mills. Thousands of extra workers were hired to help mine this coal. Many blacks from the South came to our state in hopes of finding jobs and a better way of life. Most settled near the big industrial centers of Pittsburgh and Philadelphia.

The 1920s also brought about changes in how Pennsylvanians spent their **leisure time.** Leisure time is time spent away from work. Before the 1920s, many Americans entertained themselves by reading books. Two of the most popular books in the country were written by Pennsylvanians. Owen Wister's *The Virginian*, America's first cowboy story, and Kate Douglas Wiggin's *Rebecca of Sunnybrook Farm* were read by millions of people all over the country. But during the 1920s, Americans' imaginations were captured by two new forms of entertainment: the radio and the movies.

In 1920 the first radio station in the world began to broadcast. It was station KDKA in Pittsburgh.   People

As a result of the radio, many Pennsylvanians were able to enjoy live broadcasts of baseball games.

The radio became the center of home entertainment during the 1920s and 1930s. As this family shows, people could listen to the radio while engaging in other activities.

rushed out to buy radios, which gave them a new source of entertainment. Radio shows became very popular. People could learn the news of the day almost as soon as it happened. Sports fans could listen to broadcasts of baseball games right in their own living rooms.

Movies also became a popular form of entertainment in the 1920s. America's first movie theater opened in Pittsburgh on June 19, 1905. For a few cents, people who had spent a hard day at work could relax while watching a movie at the local theater.

Conservation in Pennsylvania
Although life in Pennsylvania was improving, the state did have some serious problems to correct. One was in the area of conservation. Conservation is preserving or protecting natural resources. By the 1920s, many of Pennsylvania's large trees had been cut down for use by lumbering companies. Mills and mines **polluted** streams and rivers by dumping their wastes into the water. Pollute means "to make unclean." The polluted streams and smaller forest areas threatened Pennsylvania's wildlife.

In 1923, Gifford Pinchot became the governor of Pennsylvania. Before his election, Pinchot was the chief forester of the Forest Service, which was set up by President Theodore Roosevelt. As chief forester, Pinchot helped start a system of national forests across the country. These forests saved a large number of trees for the future. One of the largest national forests is right here in Pennsylvania. It is Allegheny National Forest.

Governor Pinchot started conservation programs in Pennsylvania. A program was started to plant new trees. Laws were passed to protect wildlife. Some of these laws set rules for hunting and fishing. Pinchot was a pioneer in trying to save the natural resources of Pennsylvania and the nation.

Pennsylvania's many lakes, rivers, and streams are favorite spots for people who enjoy fishing.

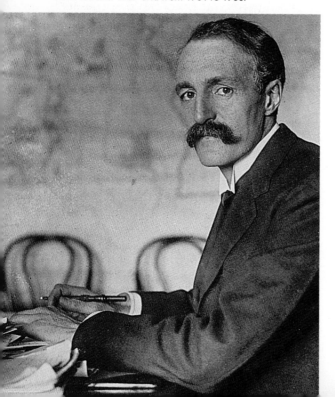

Gifford Pinchot served 2 terms as Pennsylvania's governor, from 1923 to 1927 and from 1931 to 1935.

The Great Depression   As the 1920s came to a close, Pennsylvania had another serious problem to deal with. Our state's **economy,** which was growing strong in the early 1920s, started to weaken. An economy is how a state or country uses its workers and resources to produce goods and services. Many Pennsylvania workers were forced to accept lower pay at their jobs. Other workers even lost their jobs. Pennsylvania's coal miners and farmers were hit especially hard. Both had produced more of their products than they could sell. This forced the prices of their products down. Many miners lost their jobs and many farmers had to give up their farms.

This is how some people in Pittsburgh lived during the Great Depression.

Economic problems were spreading throughout the United States. In 1929 the country was hit by a **depression.** A depression is a time when many people do not have jobs. The depression that began in 1929 was so terrible that it became known as the Great Depression. During the Great Depression, people had little money, so they did not buy much. Stores had to close because they could not sell their products. This caused factories to close because the stores could not buy their goods. As a result, factory and store workers lost their jobs. Farmers had a hard time selling their crops because people could not afford to buy them. Many farmers had to sell their farms because they could not pay their bills.

The closing of factories that made things like automobiles affected Pennsylvania's steel mills. Before the Great Depression began, the United States Steel Corporation made about 18 million tons (16.3 t) of steel. By 1932 it made only 4 million tons (3.6 t). Many workers at its mills and mines lost their jobs. Some family members even left their homes and went to other parts of the country to look for work.

During the Great Depression many people who could not afford to buy food waited in long lines called "soup lines" to get a piece of bread and a bowl of soup.

Fighting the Depression   As you can see, there was much suffering during the Great Depression. More than a million Pennsylvanians were without jobs and in great need of help.

In November of 1930, Gifford Pinchot was elected governor for a second time. He went right to work helping the people of the state. The first thing he did was to get the government of Pennsylvania to give $10 million to help the most needy people in Pennsylvania. Governor Pinchot also got money from the national government, in Washington, D.C., to start projects across the state that would give many Pennsylvanians jobs. One such project was a road-building program in **rural** areas. *Rural* means "having to do with the country, not the city." This project not only provided many needy people with jobs, but also allowed farmers to get their crops to market more easily. This helped farmers earn much-needed money.

CHECKUP

1. Where was the first radio station in the world?
2. What governor did much for conservation in Pennsylvania?
3. When did the Great Depression begin?

World War II and After

World War II   As the people of the United States were recovering from the Great Depression, some of the countries in Europe were preparing themselves for another war. In September of 1939, Germany attacked the country of Poland. This was the start of World War II. Germany and Italy again formed an alliance, but this time the Asian nation of Japan was included. The United Kingdom, France, and Russia (which was by this time known as the Soviet Union) joined forces to fight against Germany. The United States was **neutral,** or was not on any side in the war until December 7, 1941. On that date the Japanese made a surprise attack on a United States naval base at Pearl Harbor, in Hawaii. Because of this attack, our country declared war on Japan. To help Japan, Germany and Italy declared war on the United States. As a result, for the next 4 years, the United States fought on the side of the United Kingdom, France, the Soviet Union, and a number of other countries. Together these countries were called the **Allies.**

Japan's surprise attack on the United States naval base at Pearl Harbor on December 7, 1941, brought America into World War II.

Pennsylvania gave much support to the Allies during World War II. Over 1 million men and women from our state served in the armed forces. George C. Marshall, from Uniontown, Pennsylvania, was the commanding officer of the entire army. The United States Air Force was under the command of another Pennsylvanian, Henry H. Arnold, from Gladwyne. Over 100 generals and admirals came from Pennsylvania.

Our state had many military camps and training centers. Indiantown Gap, Camp Reynolds, and the Carlisle Barracks were the largest of these camps. Pennsylvania's farms produced a large amount of the food for the troops. Our mills and factories made thousands of weapons and tons of bombs. Great battleships were built in Philadelphia.

The war lasted until 1945. In the end the Allies defeated Germany, Italy, and Japan. Over 30,000 soldiers and sailors from Pennsylvania died during the war. Many others were wounded while fighting for our country.

People on the move   Many people in Pennsylvania changed the way they lived after World War II. A great number of them moved from farms to the cities. They looked for work in businesses and factories there. As Pennsylvania's cities became overcrowded,

Workers at the shipyards in Philadelphia and Chester built many ships for the American navy during World War II.

136

Marian Anderson

Pennsylvania has been the home of many famous artists and musicians. One of the greatest is the singer Marian Anderson.

Born on February 17, 1902, Marian Anderson grew up in the city of Philadelphia. Her dream was to become a concert performer. To reach this goal, she studied music and got the training she needed.

In 1939, Anderson was not allowed to sing at the leading concert hall in Washington, D.C., because she was black. When news of this reached Eleanor Roosevelt, the wife of President Franklin Roosevelt, she arranged for Marian Anderson to sing on the steps of the Lincoln Memorial. Over 70,000 people came to hear Marian Anderson sing.

Since then, Marian Anderson has had the opportunity to sing all over the world. In 1955 she became the first black person to sing with the New York Metropolitan Opera Company. Marian Anderson has also made many records. Pennsylvanians can be truly proud of this great artist from our state.

people started to move to the **suburbs.** A suburb is a smaller town or community near a large city. Soon many people were living in suburbs but working in the nearby cities. For example, many people living in Ardmore, Devon, and Paoli worked in the city of Philadelphia. A major reason why they could do this was the automobile.

After the war, thousands of people bought automobiles. With improved roads being built all over the state, people traveled more than ever before. One of the roads built at this time was the Pennsylvania Turnpike.

New immigrants   There was another change in Pennsylvania's population after World War II. A large number of European immigrants began settling in our state. Many of these immigrants had lost their homes and jobs in Europe during World War II. Most of them settled in the cities of Philadelphia and Pittsburgh.

In the 1960s and 1970s, many people from Puerto Rico came to live in Pennsylvania. Most settled in and around the city of Philadelphia. During the 1980s, a large number of people from countries such as Vietnam were forced

After World War II the suburbs around Pennsylvania's cities started to grow. Many people who live in the suburbs work in a nearby city. Do you live in a surburb?

138

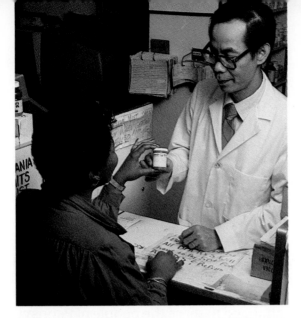

The pharmacist in the photo above immigrated to Pennsylvania from the country of Vietnam.

to leave their homes because of war. Many of these people came to live in Pennsylvania. All of these new immigrant groups are playing an important role in shaping the future of Pennsylvania.

CHECKUP

1. When did World War II begin?
2. Where were battleships built in Pennsylvania?
3. Why did many European immigrants come to Pennsylvania after World War II?

9/CHAPTER REVIEW

Some Key Terms On a piece of paper write the words missing from the sentences below. Use these words: *leisure time, depression, suburb, Allies, armistice.*

1. _____ is time spent away from work.

2. An _____ is an agreement between countries to stop fighting each other.

3. The _____ were the countries who fought against Germany, Italy, and Japan in World War II.

4. A _____ is a time when many people do not have jobs.

5. A smaller town or community near a large city is a _____.

Do Some Research Use an encyclopedia or other reference book to find the answers to the following questions.

1. Who served as governor of Pennsylvania between the two terms of Gifford Pinchot?

2. Name all of the countries that fought for the Allies during World War II.

3. How long is the Pennsylvania Turnpike?

4. Which nations made up the *Big Four* during World War II?

5. Who was President of the United States when the atomic bomb was used on two Japanese cities?

For Thought Write a paragraph or two in answer to one of the following questions.

1. How did the growth of suburbs in Pennsylvania after World War II change the way many Pennsylvanians lived?

2. How have Pennsylvania's recent immigrants improved our state?

139

State Government

┌─ VOCABULARY ─────────────────┐
state government **capitol**
local government
└──────────────────────────────┘

Kinds of government The **state government** of Pennsylvania is the government of all the people of Pennsylvania. Voters from all parts of the state elect people to represent them in Harrisburg, our state capital. A person must be a citizen of the United States, live in Pennsylvania, and be at least 18 years old to vote in Pennsylvania. Voters also choose representatives to their **local governments.** County government and city government are two kinds of local government in Pennsylvania.

Our constitution You may remember from Chapter 4 that a constitution is a set of laws by which a place is governed. We have a United States Constitution for the nation. Each of the 50 states also has its own constitution.

Over the years Pennsylvania has had five constitutions. Pennsylvania's first constitution was written in 1776. The last one was written in 1967. Each time our constitution was rewritten, it was changed to serve the people of Pennsylvania better.

The capital city Harrisburg was chosen as the capital city of Pennsylvania in 1812. Before this time, Philadelphia and Lancaster were capitals of our state.

Once Harrisburg became Pennsylvania's capital, it needed a special building called the **capitol.** The capitol is the most important building in Harrisburg. It is the building where our state leaders meet to make laws for Pennsylvania. *Capitol*, the word for the building, sounds just like *capital*, the word for the city of Harrisburg. You will notice, however, that the two words are spelled differently.

Harrisburg has had two buildings

The state capitol in Harrisburg was completed in 1906.

serve as the capitol. The first capitol was built between the years 1818 and 1822. It served as the center of Pennsylvania's state government until the building was destroyed by fire in 1897. Our present state capitol was begun in 1902 and finished in 1906. This building was designed by Joseph M. Houston and cost about $13 million to build. Our capitol includes statues made by Pennsylvania's world-famous sculptor, George Grey Barnard. It also has a beautiful dome that is 272 feet (83 m) high. The building was officially

Governor Robert Casey is the leader of the executive branch of our state government. Dick Thornburgh, former governor of Pennsylvania, was named Attorney General of the United States in 1988.

opened on October 4, 1906, with ceremonies that included a speech by the President of the United States, Theodore Roosevelt. Throughout the years this beautiful building has remained a source of pride for all Pennsylvanians.

CHECKUP

1. How old must you be to vote in Pennsylvania?
2. How many constitutions has the state of Pennsylvania had?
3. When was Harrisburg chosen as the capital city of Pennsylvania?

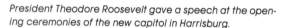

President Theodore Roosevelt gave a speech at the opening ceremonies of the new capitol in Harrisburg.

142

How Pennsylvania's State Government Works

Branches of government   Pennsylvania has three branches, or parts, in its state government. One is the **executive branch.** Another is the **legislative branch.** The third is the **judicial branch.**

Executive branch   The person who heads the executive branch of Pennsylvania's government is the governor. The governor's job is to make sure all of the state's laws are followed. The governor is elected for a term of 4 years. In Pennsylvania the governor can be elected for a second term. The governor is the leader of the state. He or she chooses the people to head nearly every department in the state.

If the governor is unable to do his or her job, the **lieutenant governor** takes over. This person is elected with the governor and helps to run the state.

Legislative branch   The laws of Pennsylvania are made by the legislative branch of government. This branch is called the **General Assembly.** The General Assembly is divided into two parts.

One part of the General Assembly is the **House of Representatives.** The House of Representatives has 203 members, one for each district in the state. The voters of each district elect a person to represent them in the state House of Representatives. Representatives are elected every 2 years.

The other part of the General Assembly is called the **Senate.** The Senate has 50 members. They are called **senators.** Each senator represents the people in his or her senatorial district. Each of these districts has about the same population. A senator is elected

Pennsylvania's General Assembly meets in this room in the capitol in Harrisburg.

How a Bill Becomes a Law

1. A member of the House of Representatives or Senate writes a bill.

2. The House of Representatives and Senate approve the bill.

3. The governor signs the bill, and it becomes a law.

4. If the governor vetoes the bill, it goes back to the House of Representatives and Senate.

5. The House of Representatives and Senate vote again. If the bill gets 2/3 of the votes, it becomes a law.

The Pennsylvania Supreme Court meets in Harrisburg. Our state supreme court is made up of one chief justice and six associate justices.

for a term of 4 years. The lieutenant governor is the person who heads the state senate.

The job of the legislative branch is to make laws for Pennsylvania. To make a law, both parts of the General Assembly must approve a **bill.** A bill is a possible law. If a bill is approved, it is sent to the governor. If the governor also approves the bill, he or she signs it, and the bill becomes a law. But the governor might decide to **veto,** or not approve, the bill. When this happens, the General Assembly still has a chance to make the bill a law. If two thirds of the members of both the House of Representatives and the Senate approve the bill, it becomes a law. This means that 156 representatives and 34 senators must vote for the vetoed bill.

Judicial branch   The branch of government that explains the laws is called the judicial branch. This branch makes certain that people who break the law are punished. It does this through a system of courts.

The state supreme court is the highest court in the state. It is made up of a chief justice, or judge, and six associate justices. These seven judges are elected by the voters in our state. Each judge is elected for a 10-year term of office.

CHECKUP

1. What are the two parts of Pennsylvania's General Assembly?
2. Who signs a bill into law?
3. How many state supreme court justices are there in Pennsylvania?

Local Government

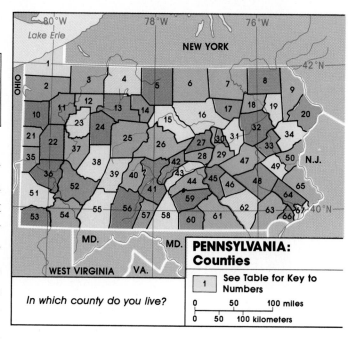

PENNSYLVANIA: Counties

| 1 | See Table for Key to Numbers |

0   50   100 miles

0   50   100 kilometers

In which county do you live?

County government   Pennsylvania is divided into 67 counties. Each one has a **county seat**. A county seat is the town or city where the county government is located. The county courthouse and office buildings are found in the county seat. What is the name of your county and county seat?

Each county is governed by a **board of county commissioners.** The board is a group of three people. They are elected by the county's voters every 4 years. It is their job to make the laws for the county. They also see that these laws are carried out. The county government gives many other services to people. It keeps records of marriages, births, and deaths. It has a system of county courts and a police force. Counties also take care of some roads. Can you name any other services of county governments?

PENNSYLVANIA COUNTIES

County	No.	County	No.	County	No.
Adams	60	Elk	13	Montgomery	64
Allegheny	36	Erie	1	Montour	30
Armstrong	37	Fayette	54	Northampton	50
Beaver	35	Forest	12	Northumberland	29
Bedford	56	Franklin	58	Perry	44
Berks	48	Fulton	57	Philadelphia	67
Blair	40	Greene	53	Pike	20
Bradford	7	Huntingdon	41	Potter	5
Bucks	65	Indiana	38	Schuylkill	47
Butler	22	Jefferson	24	Snyder	28
Cambria	39	Juniata	43	Somerset	55
Cameron	14	Lackawanna	19	Sullivan	17
Carbon	33	Lancaster	62	Susquehanna	8
Centre	26	Lawrence	21	Tioga	6
Chester	63	Lebanon	46	Union	27
Clarion	23	Lehigh	49	Venango	11
Clearfield	25	Luzerne	32	Warren	3
Clinton	15	Lycoming	16	Washington	51
Columbia	31	McKean	4	Wayne	9
Crawford	2	Mercer	10	Westmoreland	52
Cumberland	59	Mifflin	42	Wyoming	18
Dauphin	45	Monroe	34	York	61
Delaware	66				

City government   There are about 50 cities in our state. Each city in Pennsylvania has a government. Like the counties, city governments provide many services. These include police and fire protection.

Pennsylvania also has communities known as **townships** and **boroughs** (bėr′ ōs). There are over 1,500 townships and almost 1,000 boroughs in our

W. Wilson Goode

W. Wilson Goode became the 126th mayor of Philadelphia on January 2, 1984. He is the first black person to hold this important position. Before becoming mayor, Goode worked for 18 years for the people of Philadelphia.

Goode and his family moved to Philadelphia from North Carolina when he was 15 years old. After serving in the army, Goode returned to his southwest Philadelphia neighborhood. He became president of the Paschall Betterment League. This league helped to improve recreational facilities and get summer jobs for youths.

From 1966 to 1978, Goode worked for the Philadelphia Council for Community Advancement. Through his efforts, Philadelphia developed one of the best housing programs in the United States.

Goode's leadership qualities and hard work led to his appointment as managing director of the city of Philadelphia in 1979. As managing director, he worked to improve city spending and services provided to the citizens of Philadelphia.

In November 1983, Goode was elected to be the mayor of Philadelphia. As mayor, Goode is working hard to rebuild Philadelphia's neighborhoods and

economy, to make the city safe and clean, and to provide help for the needy. Although all of these problems are not yet solved, Philadelphians can be sure that W. Wilson Goode will continue to work hard to keep Philadelphia the great city it is.

state. Like cities, they provide many basic services for their citizens. These services are paid for with taxes people pay to the government. Do you live in a city, a township, or a borough?

CHECKUP

1. What is a county seat?
2. What kinds of services do county governments provide for the people of the county?
3. About how many townships and boroughs are there in Pennsylvania?

147

Pennsylvania and the National Government

In the nation   As citizens of the United States, Pennsylvania voters also send people to represent our state in Congress. Congress is the legislative branch of our national government. It meets in our nation's capital, Washington, D.C. The Congress of the United States is divided into two parts. One part is known as the House of Representatives. The other part is the Senate.

Each state in the United States has two representatives in the United States Senate. These people are called senators. They are chosen for a 6-year term. Each senator represents his or her entire state.

The number of representatives from a state in the House of Representatives depends on how many people live in the state. States with large populations have more representatives. States with smaller populations have fewer representatives. Pennsylvania has 23 representatives in the House of Representatives. They serve 2-year terms.

The Pennsylvania representatives represent the people living in their **congressional districts.** A congressional district is a division of the state according to population. Each of Pennsylvania's 23 congressional districts elects one person to serve in the House of Representatives. Only three states have more representatives than Pennsylvania.

The United States Senate has two senators from each state. Pennsylvania's two senators are John Heinz (left) and Arlen Specter.

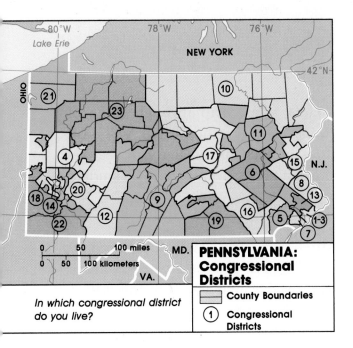

PENNSYLVANIA: Congressional Districts

County Boundaries

① Congressional Districts

In which congressional district do you live?

Pennsylvania voters also help to choose the President of the United States. Presidential elections are held every 4 years, in the month of November. Any citizen of the United States, 18 years old or older, may vote in a Presidential election.

CHECKUP

1. What is the legislative branch of our national government called?
2. How long is a senator's term in office?
3. How many representatives does Pennsylvania have in the national House of Representatives?

10/CHAPTER REVIEW

Some Key Terms On a piece of paper write the words missing from the sentences below. Use these words: *capitol, legislative branch, executive branch, veto,* and *board of county commissioners.*

1. The group that governs a county is called the _____ .

2. The branch of government that makes laws is the _____ .

3. A _____ is the building where the people who make laws meet.

4. The _____ of government sees to it that the laws are followed.

5. The governor can decide to _____ , or not approve, a bill.

Do Some Research Use an encyclopedia or other reference book to find the answers to the following questions.

1. Who is your representative in the state House of Representatives?

2. Who is your state senator?

3. Who is the president of the United States Senate?

For Thought Write a paragraph or two in answer to one of the following questions.

1. Why do we need state government?

2. Why do we need local government?

3. How do state and local governments differ?

A Look at Pennsylvania's Cities

VOCABULARY

urban area	service
import	industry
export	resort

Why people live in cities Where do you live? Do you live in a large city or in one of its suburbs? Do you live in an apartment or in a house? Maybe you live on a farm.

Pennsylvania has many different kinds of places where people live. But most Pennsylvanians live in cities or **urban areas.** An urban area is made up of a large city and its suburbs.

Can you think of reasons why so many people live in cities? If your answer is that there are many jobs in cities, you are right. But there are many other things to do in cities. You can visit museums, tall buildings, parks, and zoos. You can watch professional sports teams. You can see plays and hear concerts. You are close to stores and schools.

Let's take a trip through some of Pennsylvania's cities. We will visit cities in each of the five physical regions of Pennsylvania that you studied in Chapter 2.

Cities of the Atlantic Coastal Plain The largest city on the Atlantic Coastal Plain in Pennsylvania is Philadelphia. More than 1,600,000 people live in this city. Philadelphia is the most populated city in the state and the fifth most populated in the nation. Many of the smaller towns and cities near Philadelphia are considered part of the Philadelphia urban area. The Philadelphia urban area has about 4,800,000 people in it. It includes towns and suburbs such as Norristown, Germantown, and Upper Darby in Pennsylvania, and Pennsauken in New Jersey.

Because of Philadelphia's location on the Delaware River, the city has one of the busiest ports in the United States. Many **imports** and **exports** are shipped through the port of Philadelphia. Crude oil is an import that comes

Pennsylvania's cities are fun places to live in and to visit.

150

into the port of Philadelphia. Imports are goods shipped into a country. Exports are goods shipped out of a country. Philadelphia's oil refineries then turn this crude oil into gasoline and many other products. Farm products and coal are some products that are exported from Pennsylvania.

Philadelphia is one of our nation's leading industrial cities. Besides oil refining, Philadelphia industries include clothing, food processing, and printing. Many of our nation's large banks and insurance companies also have their main offices in Philadelphia. These industries are called **service industries.** A service industry provides a service to people rather than producing goods.

In addition to the over 1 million people who live and work in Philadelphia, millions of people visit the city's many tourist attractions and attend its colleges and universities. Independence Hall and the Liberty Bell are visited by people from all over the world. The Philadelphia Museum of Art, the Franklin Institute Science Museum and Planetarium, Fairmont Park, and the Philadelphia Zoo are also popular tourist spots. Philadelphia is also the home of 30 colleges and universities, including the University of Pennsylvania, Temple University, and St. Joseph's College.

Philadelphia has a variety of professional sports teams that provide thousands of fans with year-round entertainment. The National Basketball Association's 76ers and the National Hockey League's Flyers provide excitement at the Spectrum; the National Football League's Eagles and baseball's Phillies provide the action at Veterans Stadium.

Banks provide many services to the people of Pennsylvania. Banking is one type of service industry.

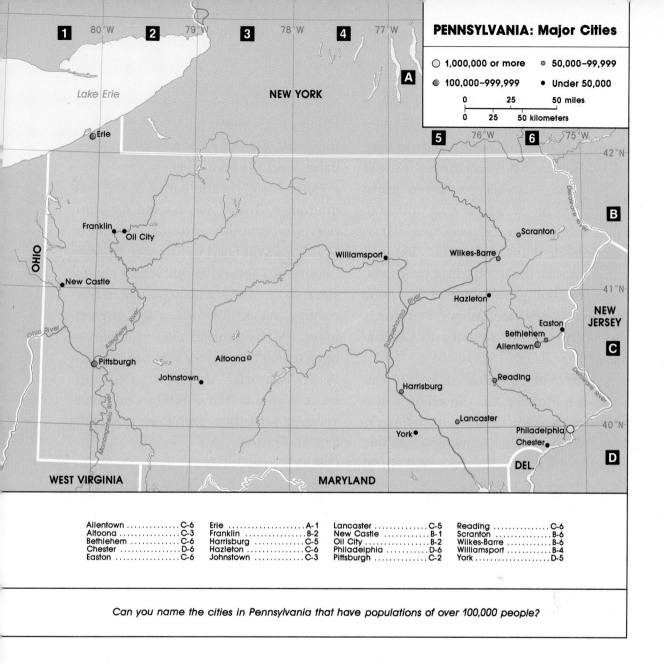

PENNSYLVANIA: Major Cities

○ 1,000,000 or more ◐ 50,000–99,999

◑ 100,000–999,999 • Under 50,000

Can you name the cities in Pennsylvania that have populations of over 100,000 people?

Another large city on the Atlantic Coastal Plain is Chester. Find Chester on the map above. It has a population of almost 46,000 people and is part of the Philadelphia urban area. As you read in Chapter 4, Chester was once the Swedish settlement of Upland. Because of its location on the Delaware River, Chester quickly became a leading port. Today its most important industry is oil refining.

Cities of the Piedmont   There are two large cities in the Piedmont region of our state. They are Lancaster and York.

Lancaster is an important manufacturing and farming city located between Philadelphia and our state capital, Harrisburg. Built on the richest soil in the state, Lancaster's farms grow record crops of grain and tobacco. Their dairy herds produce large amounts of dairy products. Lancaster's factories make building products, electrical equipment, watches, floor tiles, and heavy machinery. Printing is also an important industry in Lancaster.

A little over 20 miles (32 km) to the west of Lancaster, on the edge of the Piedmont region, is the city of York. York developed as a trading center. Today, York is a center for agricultural products and machinery.

Cities among the ridges and valleys There are many cities in Pennsylvania's Ridge and Valley Region. The largest of these are Allentown, Altoona, Bethlehem, Easton, Harrisburg, Hazleton, Reading, Scranton, Wilkes-Barre, and Williamsport.

Harrisburg, on the banks of the Susquehanna River, was named for John Harris, who built a trading post there in 1718. As you read in Chapter 10, Harrisburg has served as our state's capital since 1812. Over 15,000 people in Harrisburg work for our state government. Many tourists also visit Harrisburg to see the capitol and the William Penn Memorial Museum. This museum contains many exhibits on Pennsylvania's history and Pennsylvanian arts and crafts.

Harrisburg is also a manufacturing center. Steel and steel products, clothing, meat products, and lumber products are made there. Harrisburg is a printing and publishing center for the state.

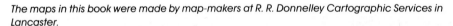

The maps in this book were made by map-makers at R. R. Donnelley Cartographic Services in Lancaster.

There are two large urban areas in the Ridge and Valley Region. The first of these is the Allentown-Bethlehem-Easton area. These three important cities are located between the Lehigh and Delaware rivers, in eastern Pennsylvania. There are 200,000 people living in this urban area. Many work in Bethlehem's steel plants or in Allentown's textile mills. Bethlehem is also the home of Lehigh University and Moravian College. Factories in Easton make textiles, leather, paper, and clothing.

Moravian College is located in Bethlehem. It is one of the many good colleges found in Pennsylvania.

Skiing is a popular winter sport. Many people enjoy skiing in Pennsylvania's Pocono Mountains.

Scranton, Wilkes-Barre, and Hazleton, located in the northeastern part of our state, make up another important urban area. There are many manufacturing plants in this area that make coal products, metal items, furniture, and textiles. Scranton is also a short distance from many of Pennsylvania's **resorts** in the Pocono Mountains. A resort is a place that people go to for recreation and entertainment. Thousands of people visit Pocono Mountains resorts each year.

155

Reading, with a population of about 79,000 people, is one of our state's largest cities. Reading is a manufacturing center. Factories making steel, paper, clothing, and heavy machinery line the Schuylkill River, which flows through the city. Reading is also an arts center for the region. It has a fine art gallery and museum. The Reading Public Museum and Arts Council has many different exhibits that include Pennsylvania-German art and objects once used by Pennsylvania's Indians.

Two other cities in the Ridge and Valley Region are Altoona and Williamsport. Altoona is on the western edge of the Ridge and Valley Region. It is a railroad center. Many of Altoona's buildings were once places where trains were repaired. Williamsport's industries produce aircraft engines and parts, leather goods, paper, and textiles. Williamsport is also the home of Lycoming College. The borough of State College, also located in the Ridge and Valley Region, is the home of Pennsylvania State University.

Cities of the Allegheny Plateau
Pittsburgh is the largest city on the Allegheny Plateau. It is the second most populated city in the state, with over 420,000 people. Pittsburgh's urban area population is about 2,300,000 people. In a study completed in 1985, Pittsburgh was rated as the best city in the United States to live in.

Pittsburgh is an industrial city. One-fifth of the iron and steel made in the United States comes from Pittsburgh.

Pennsylvania State University is one of the best universities in the country.

The Carnegie Museum of Natural History is famous for its collection of dinosaur skeletons.

Aluminum, glass, electrical, petroleum, and chemical products are also made in Pittsburgh.

As you have learned, Pittsburgh is located where the Allegheny and Monongahela rivers meet and form the Ohio River. These rivers provide an excellent transportation system for Pittsburgh's products. The port of Pittsburgh is the busiest inland port in the United States. The city also has good railroad, highway, and air transportation systems.

Pittsburgh is the cultural and educational center of western Pennsylvania. The Pittsburgh Symphony Orchestra and the city's opera and ballet companies perform for thousands of people each year. The Buhl Planetarium, the Pittsburgh Zoo, and the Carnegie Museum of Natural History also attract many visitors. The Carnegie Museum of Natural History includes the world's best-preserved dinosaur skeleton. Nine colleges and universities are found in the city, including the University of Pittsburgh and the Carnegie-Mellon Institute.

The people of Pittsburgh are also proud of their professional sports teams. The football Steelers, baseball Pirates, and hockey Penguins all have large followings. The basketball and football teams of the University of Pittsburgh also have many fans in the city.

The second largest city on the Allegheny Plateau is Johnstown. Coal mining and steelmaking are important industries in Johnstown. Johnstown is located on the Conemaugh River. Some of the worst floods in Pennsylvania history have happened in Johnstown. The great floods of 1889, 1937, and 1977 caused great damage throughout the city.

New Castle, Oil City, and Franklin are three other cities found in the northwestern part of the plateau. New Castle is the largest of the three. The two other cities, Oil City and Franklin, form an urban area. This was the area where oil was first discovered in Pennsylvania. The two cities have since been a center for the oil-refining industry in Pennsylvania.

Workers at the port of Erie load ships with goods to be shipped to other parts of the country.

The Erie Plain   Erie is the only city found on the Erie Plain. The city of Erie is located in the northwestern corner of the state, on the shore of Lake Erie. Erie acts as Pennsylvania's port on the Great Lakes for shipping coal, iron, grain, lumber, and many other manufactured goods. Tourist areas such as Erie Harbor, Presque Isle State Park, and the coastline of Lake Erie attract thousands of visitors each year.

One of the many activities enjoyed by vacationers on Lake Erie is sailing. Have you ever been on a sailboat?

CHECKUP

1. What is the largest city in Pennsylvania?
2. Where is the busiest inland port in the United States?
3. What is the only city on the Erie Plain?

The Environment and Pollution

┌─ VOCABULARY ─────────────┐
│ **acid rain**   **pesticide**
│ **landfill**   **toxic waste**
│ **biology**
└──────────────────────────┘

Environment   As you remember from Chapter 3, our environment is all of the things around us, such as water, land, animals, plants, and air. A polluted environment can have bad effects on your health. Most Pennsylvanians are working hard to rid our state of all types of pollution.

Air pollution   Air pollution is a problem in most states, especially in urban areas. Smoke from businesses and factories that burn coal and oil and exhaust fumes from cars, buses, and trucks combine to make air pollution. Polluted air does not smell good. If it is bad enough, air pollution can make you ill.

Pennsylvanians have been fighting to get rid of air pollution in our state. In the 1960s and 1970s, our General Assembly passed laws making it a crime to pollute the air. The most effective of these laws was the State Air Pollution Control Act. Because of this law and the hard work of many industries, Pennsylvania's air is among the cleanest in the nation.

Water pollution   Water pollution is caused by allowing waste to get into our lakes, streams, and rivers. Waste is material that is of no use. One kind of waste that causes water pollution comes from Pennsylvania's coal mines. For years, water ran through the old mines. Chemicals used in the mines, such as iron, sulfur, and acids, mixed in with the water. The water flowed from the mines into nearby streams and rivers, turning them yellow and killing many plants and animals. Many other mills and factories dumped their wastes into rivers. This not only polluted the water, but also killed many fish.

These students are helping to fight pollution by cleaning up a section of their community.

Rachel Carson

There are many ways to help keep Pennsylvania's environment clean. One Pennsylvanian, Rachel Carson, wrote books to make people aware of the serious problem of pollution.

Rachel Carson was born and raised in Springdale, Pennsylvania. She went to the Pennsylvania College for Women to study English. While in college she changed her course of study to **biology.** Biology is the study of living things. Carson became very interested in studying the plant and animal life of the sea. After graduating from college she worked for the United States Fish and Wildlife Service.

Carson also wrote four books. Her first book was called *Under the Sea Wind* (1941). But it was for her fourth and last book that she received the most attention. The title of this book was *Silent Spring. Silent Spring* warned people that the use of **pesticides** was killing many birds and fish by poisoning their food. A pesticide is a chemical

used to kill certain insects. These insects are usually harmful to people or crops.

Rachel Carson died on April 14, 1964. Her book helped to show the need for laws to limit the use of pesticides. All Pennsylvanians can be proud of Rachel Carson.

During the 1960s, Pennsylvania passed strict laws to stop water pollution. Old unused mines were sealed shut. This kept the polluted water from escaping into streams and rivers. Strip mines had to be covered with soil and replanted with grass after the coal was removed. This kept the rainwater from mixing with the chemicals in the open strip mines. Industries, cities, and towns had to make sure their waste was safe before it was put into the waterways.

One serious pollution problem still

exists. Certain chemicals released into the air by some power plants mix with precipitation. Together they form something called **acid rain.** Acid rain pollutes both the soil and the water when it falls to the earth.

Soil pollution   A third kind of pollution is found in the soil. One source of this kind of pollution is the trash and garbage that we produce. Each year, cities and towns have to find a way to get rid of the thousands of tons of garbage and trash they collect. The usual way is to bury it in places called **landfills.** The material is put into long ditches and covered with soil. The problem is that sometimes material from the garbage gets into water systems used by people for drinking and washing.

The most serious type of soil pollution is called **toxic waste.** Toxic waste is very dangerous chemicals and special products from factories that are buried or stored in the soil. Some of them are deadly poisons. Some are so poisonous that just touching them can make a person break out in a rash or become ill. How to store toxic waste safely is the number one problem in soil conservation today.

Nuclear pollution   A special pollution problem can be caused by nuclear

The Three Mile Island nuclear power plant is located near Middletown, Pennsylvania.

energy. Nuclear energy can be used to heat water into steam. This steam is then used to make electricity. People do not agree that this way of making electricity is safe. Any accidents can cause a serious pollution problem.

In 1979 a major nuclear reactor accident occurred at the Three Mile Island nuclear power plant near Middletown, Pennsylvania. The reactor had to be closed for repairs and many people in the area were forced to leave their homes for a short time. Effects on the people and the environment of this area are still being studied.

CHECKUP

1. What law was passed in Pennsylvania to fight air pollution?
2. What are some causes of water pollution?
3. What is the most serious kind of soil pollution?

The People of Pennsylvania

Pennsylvanians help shape American history As you finish your study of Pennsylvania, try to remember some of the people from Pennsylvania that have helped make the United States a great country. People such as Benjamin Franklin, Robert Fulton, Lucretia Mott, James Buchanan, George Westinghouse, Marian Anderson, and many others have all shaped American history. Today, Pennsylvanians from all different fields are still helping America grow.

People making a better government Since the end of World War II, the role of minorities and women in our state government has continued to grow. In 1952, Genevieve Blatt became the first woman to be elected to a statewide office. Nine years later Anne X. Alpren was appointed as the first woman justice on the state supreme court. In 1971, C. DeLores Tucker became Pennsylvania's **Secretary of State.** The Secretary of State is responsible for keeping all official state records. Secretary Tucker was both the first woman and the first black to

K. Leroy Irvis was the first black to be elected as Pennsylvania's Speaker of the House of Representatives. He was reelected to this position in 1987.

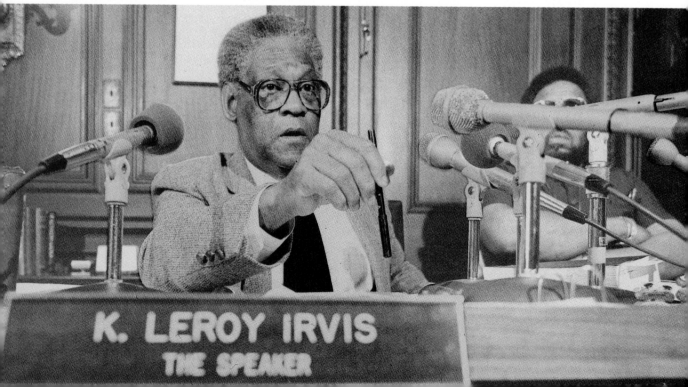

K. LEROY IRVIS
THE SPEAKER

Tales of the South Pacific by James Michener was written about islands in the South Pacific Ocean like the one shown in this picture.

hold this important office. In that same year Robert Nix, Jr., became the state's first black justice on the state supreme court. Later in the 1970s, K. Leroy Irvis, a member of the state House of Representatives, became the first black to be elected as **Speaker of the House.** The Speaker of the House is the leading member of the House of Representatives. Mr. Irvis was re-elected to this position in 1987. All of these Pennsylvanians have worked hard to make our state government work better.

Pennsylvanians in art and literature There are many kinds of literature. **Novels,** plays, and poetry are different kinds of literature. A novel is a story with characters and a plot. Several Pennsylvanians have made important contributions to literature since World War II.

Two of America's most famous **contemporary,** or recent, authors are from Pennsylvania. Both James Michener and John Updike are known all over the world for their novels.

James Michener grew up in Doylestown, Pennsylvania. Many of Michener's novels are **historical fiction.** Historical fiction is a story that combines historical facts with imaginary people and events. Some of Michener's novels are *Tales of the South Pacific, Hawaii, Poland,* and *Space.*

John Updike was born in Shillington, Pennsylvania. He is considered to be one of America's most talented writers. *Rabbit Run* (1960) and *A Month of Sundays* (1975) are two of his many novels about the lives of middle-class Americans. Updike also wrote a number of poems and short stories.

A contemporary artist from Pennsylvania has also become world famous in his field. Andrew Wyeth was born and raised in Chadds Ford, Pennsylvania. Many of Wyeth's paintings are of rural Pennsylvania. People from all over the world have discovered the beauty of Pennsylvania through the paintings of Andrew Wyeth.

Entertainers and sports figures of Pennsylvania   In the years after World War II, more Americans than ever before entertained themselves by going to the movies. The popularity of movies made **celebrities** out of many of the actors and actresses that starred in the movies. A celebrity is a famous person. Some of these celebrities came from Pennsylvania.

Andrew Wyeth painted many pictures of the Pennsylvania countryside.

Grace Kelly was born in Philadelphia in 1929. After studying acting in New York City, she went on to star in movies such as *High Noon* and *Dial M for Murder.* In 1956, Kelly left acting to marry Prince Rainier III, from the country of Monaco. As princess of Monaco she devoted her time to her family and charities. Princess Grace died in an automobile accident in 1982.

Three famous actors were also born in Pennsylvania. Jimmy Stewart, born in Indiana, Pennsylvania, starred in over 70 movies. In 1940 he won the Academy Award as the year's best actor for his role in the movie *The Philadelphia Story.* Gene Kelly, born in Pittsburgh, is known as one of America's greatest dancers. He starred in a number of movies including *Singing in the Rain.* Bill Cosby, born in Philadelphia, is a famous comedian. Cosby is known more for his television roles than for his movies. *The Bill Cosby Show,* and his most recent television program, *The Cosby Show,* have both been successful.

Music is another popular form of entertainment. Again, Pennsylvanians have made important contributions to contemporary music. Every year, people from all over the world come to Philadelphia and Pittsburgh to hear each city's symphony orchestra.

Many people also go to theaters to see

Bill Cosby is one of many famous entertainers who come from Pennsylvania. Can you name any others?

musical plays. In a musical play, the actors and actresses sing some of their lines. One of the most famous American musical play writers, Oscar Hammerstein, lived in Doylestown, Pennsylvania. He became part of the famous team of musical play writers known as Rodgers and Hammerstein.

Together, he and Richard Rodgers wrote such musicals as *Oklahoma!* and *The Sound of Music*. Many other musical entertainers have come from Pennsylvania. These entertainers include Nelson Eddy, Perry Como, Bobby Vinton, and Mario Lanza.

Pennsylvanians have always enjoyed suporting our state's many teams. Many of the past and present athletes and coaches from Pennsylvania teams have combined successful careers with helping the people and communities of our state. Some of these sports celebrities are: Julius Erving, of the Philadelphia 76ers; Terry Bradshaw, of the Pittsburgh Steelers; Mike Schmidt, of the Philadelphia Phillies; Willie Stargell, of the Pittsburgh Pirates; and Penn State football coach Joe Paterno. Can you name any other Pennsylvania sports celebrities?

Pennsylvania and you   You have learned a great deal about Pennsylvania. You have read about the great variety of people in our state. You know something about Pennsylvania's past and its present.

You are also part of the story of Pennsylvania. You are our state's future. In the future you will have to make important decisions that will affect life in our state. You will work with others to solve our state's problems. Your study of Pennsylvania's history and geography will help you be a better Pennsylvanian today and in the future.

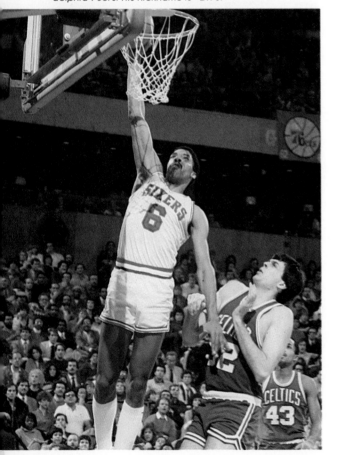

Julius Erving was a popular basketball player for the Philadelphia 76ers. His nickname is "Dr. J."

CHECKUP

1. Who was the first black Speaker of the House of Representatives in Pennsylvania?
2. What famous American actress from Pennsylvania married the prince of Monaco in 1956?
3. What are musical plays?

166

We can all be proud of our great state — Pennsylvania!

II/CHAPTER REVIEW

Some Key Terms On a piece of paper write the words missing from the sentences below. Use these words: *Philadelphia, Erie, Pittsburgh, toxic waste, urban area.*

1. _____ is the city that has the busiest inland port in the United States.

2. _____ is dangerous chemicals and special products from factories that is stored or buried in the soil.

3. The city that is Pennsylvania's port for the Great Lakes is _____.

4. _____ is the largest city in Pennsylvania.

5. An _____ is made up of a large city and its suburbs.

Do Some Research Use an encyclopedia or other reference book to find the answers to the following questions.

1. Which cities in the United States have larger populations than Philadelphia?

2. Under which Pennsylvania governor did the State Air Pollution Control Act begin?

3. What are the positive and negative effects of nuclear energy?

For Thought Write a paragraph or two in answer to one of the following questions.

1. Why do so many people vacation at Pennsylvania's Pocono Mountains resorts?

2. How can Pennsylvania solve its environmental problems?

UNIT 4/REVIEW

KEY FACTS

1. Philadelphia is the largest city in Pennsylvania.

2. Pittsburgh is the second largest city in Pennsylvania.

3. Erie is Pennsylvania's port on the Great Lakes.

4. Harrisburg is the capital of Pennsylvania and a manufacturing center.

5. Lancaster has the most productive farms in Pennsylvania.

6. Acid rain and toxic waste are the two main problems for Pennsylvania's environment.

7. Since World War II, minorities have taken an active role in Pennsylvania state government.

VOCABULARY QUIZ

Write the numbers 1 through 10 on a piece of paper. Match each term with its definition.

a. urban area f. acid rain
b. import g. landfill
c. export h. toxic waste
d. biology i. literature
e. resort j. service industry

1. A product shipped out of a country

2. A place people go to for recreation and entertainment

3. A large city surrounded by suburbs and towns

4. A mixture of chemicals and precipitation that falls to the ground

5. The study of living things

6. A product shipped into a country

7. A business that helps people in some way

8. Dangerous chemicals and poisons stored in the soil

9. All of the writings of a certain time period

10. A place where trash and garbage are buried

REVIEW QUESTIONS

1. Why do so many tourists visit Philadelphia?

2. What is manufactured in the urban area of Scranton, Wilkes-Barre, and Hazleton?

3. What two rivers meet in Pittsburgh and form the Ohio River?

ACTIVITIES

1. Plan a trip across Pennsylvania. What cities would you like to visit? What would you see in each city? Write about your imaginary trip in a report. Read your report to your classmates.

2. Search through old magazines and newspapers for pictures showing pollution. You can also draw pictures about pollution. Paste the pictures and drawings on a large piece of posterboard. Make an anti-pollution display for your school library.

READING A MILEAGE TABLE

WHAT IS A MILEAGE TABLE?

A table is a fast way to organize facts. The table below shows how far it is between some cities in Pennsylvania. It is called a mileage table.

Suppose you wanted to go from Philadelphia to Pittsburgh. Put a finger on Philadelphia in the left column. Put a finger of your other hand on Pittsburgh in the bottom row. Now move both fingers, one up and one across, until they meet. They should meet at 295. It is 295 miles (475 km) between the two cities.

SKILLS PRACTICE

It takes a little practice to read a mileage table. Soon it will be easy for you. Practice your table-reading skills by reading the table and answering these questions.

1. How many miles is it from Stroudsburg to Erie?
2. Which two cities are farthest apart? Look for the largest number on the table, and then move one finger down to the name of the city and one across to the name of the second city.
3. Which city is closest to Erie?

MILEAGE TABLE

	Bedford	Easton	Erie	Gettysburg	Harrisburg	New Castle	Philadelphia	Pittsburgh	Reading	Scranton	State College	Stroudsburg	Uniontown	Warren	Williamsport
Bedford		190	215	80	95	145	195	95	150	210	75	205	85	180	135
Easton	190		350	135	95	315	55	285	55	60	170	25	265	285	120
Erie	215	350		265	260	85	365	125	315	290	175	320	175	60	240
Gettysburg	80	135	265		40	225	115	175	85	155	115	150	160	220	125
Harrisburg	95	95	260	40		240	105	190	55	120	85	110	175	210	85
New Castle	145	315	85	225	240		340	50	290	290	160	305	95	105	205
Philadelphia	195	55	365	125	105	340		295	55	120	195	80	280	315	170
Pittsburgh	95	285	125	175	190	50	295		245	280	135	290	45	120	195
Reading	150	55	315	85	55	290	55	245		90	140	70	230	265	105
Scranton	210	60	290	155	120	290	120	280	90		140	40	290	230	80
State College	75	170	175	115	85	160	195	135	140	140		150	140	120	65
Stroudsburg	205	25	320	150	110	305	80	290	70	40	150		285	270	115
Uniontown	85	265	175	160	175	95	280	45	230	290	140	285		175	200
Warren	180	285	60	220	210	105	315	120	265	230	120	270	175		165
Williamsport	135	120	240	125	85	205	170	195	105	80	65	115	200	165	

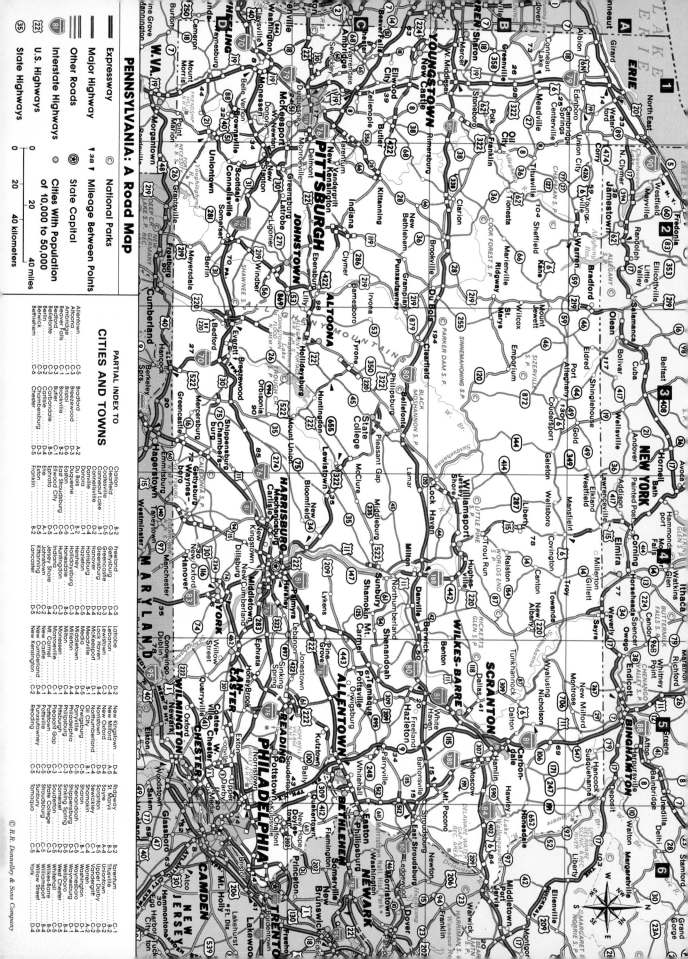

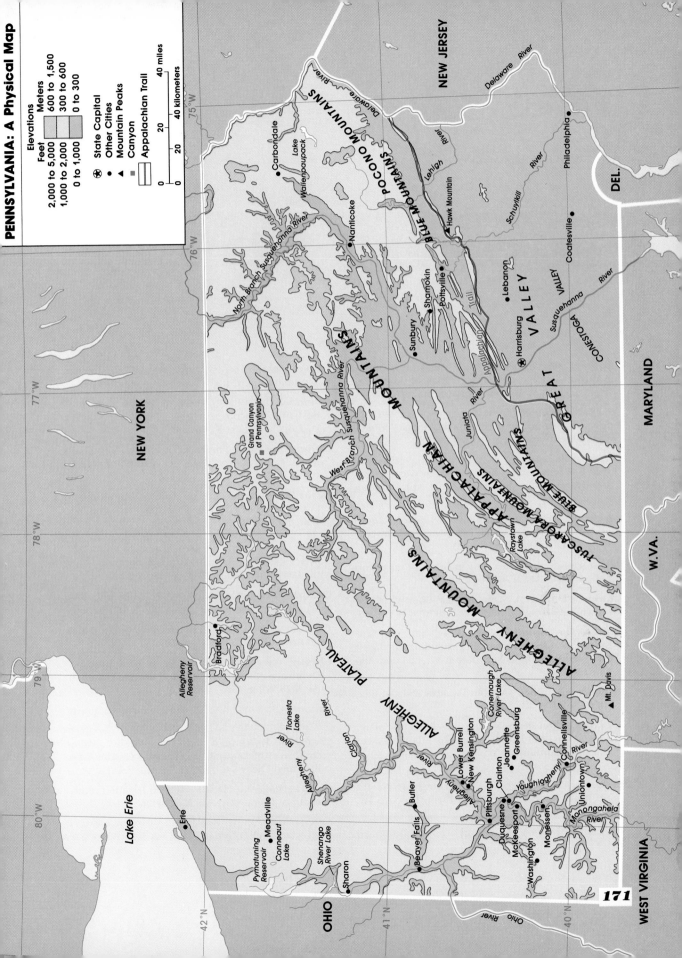

PENNSYLVANIA: A Physical Map

Elevations

Feet	Meters
2,000 to 5,000	600 to 1,500
1,000 to 2,000	300 to 600
0 to 1,000	0 to 300

⊛ State Capital
• Other Cities
▲ Mountain Peaks
■ Canyon
▬ Appalachian Trail

NEW JERSEY

NEW YORK

OHIO

MARYLAND

DEL.

W.VA.

WEST VIRGINIA

Lake Erie

Delaware River

Lehigh River

Schuylkill River

Susquehanna River

Conestoga River

Juniata River

North Branch Susquehanna River

West Branch Susquehanna River

Allegheny Reservoir

Tionesta Lake

Allegheny River

Clarion River

Conemaugh River Lake

Raystown Lake

Youghiogheny River

Monongahela River

Ohio River

Pymatuning Reservoir

Conneaut Lake

Shenango River Lake

Lake Wallenpaupack

POCONO MOUNTAINS

BLUE MOUNTAINS

BLUE MOUNTAINS

APPALACHIAN MOUNTAINS

TUSCARORA MOUNTAINS

ALLEGHENY MOUNTAINS

ALLEGHENY PLATEAU

GREAT VALLEY

Grand Canyon of Pennsylvania

Hawk Mountain

▲ Mt. Davis

Philadelphia
Coatesville
Lebanon
Harrisburg ⊛
Pottsville
Shamokin
Sunbury
Nanticoke
Carbondale
Bradford
Erie
Meadville
Sharon
Butler
Beaver Falls
Washington
Monessen
McKeesport
Duquesne
Pittsburgh
Clairton
Jeannette
Greensburg
New Kensington
Lower Burrell
Connellsville
Uniontown

75°W
76°W
77°W
78°W
79°W
80°W

42°N
41°N
40°N

0 20 40 miles
0 20 40 kilometers

GAZETTEER

The Gazetteer is a geographical dictionary. It shows latitude and longitude for cities and certain other places. Latitude and longitude are shown to the nearest degree in this form: (36°N/118°W). This means "36 degrees north latitude and 118 degrees west longitude." The page reference tells where each entry may be found on a map.

Key to Pronunciation

a	hat, cap						
ā	age, face	i	it, pin	ou	house, out	zh	measure, seizure
ã	care, air	ī	ice, five	sh	she, rush	ə	represents:
ä	father, far	ng	long, bring	th	thin, both	a	in about
ch	child, much	o	hot, rock	TH	then, smooth	e	in taken
e	let, best	ō	open, go	u	cup, butter	i	in pencil
ē	equal, see	ô	order, all	ù	full, put	o	in lemon
èr	term, learn	oi	oil, voice	ü	rule, move	u	in circus

This Key to Pronunciation is from *Scott, Foresman Intermediate Dictionary*, by E.L. Thorndike and Clarence L. Barnhart. Copyright © 1983, by Scott, Foresman and Company. Reprinted by permission.

Allegheny Mountains (al ə gā′ nē moun′ tənz). Mountain range on eastern edge of Allegheny Plateau. Part of Appalachian Mountains. p. 171.

Allegheny National Forest (al ə gā′ nē na′ shən əl for′ əst). Area of forests in northwestern Pennsylvania, south and east of Warren. p. 5.

Allegheny Plateau (al ə gā′ nē pla tō′). High land that has hills and shallow valleys, in western and northern Pennsylvania. Part of Appalachian Mountains. p. 25.

Allegheny River (al ə gā′ nē riv′ er). Flows south and meets the Monongahela River to form the Ohio River at Pittsburgh. p. 25.

Allentown (al′ ən toun). City in Lehigh County, on Lehigh River. (41°N/76°W). p. 153.

Altoona (al tü′ nə). City in Blair County, in the bituminous coal-mining area. (40°N/78°W). p.153.

Appalachian Mountains (ap ə la′ chən moun′ tənz). Ranges of mountains extending northeast and southwest between eastern Canada and Alabama. p. 171.

Ardmore (ärd′ môr). A suburb west of Philadelphia. (40°N/75°W). p. 23.

Atlantic Coastal Plain (at lan′ tik kōs təl plān). Low, almost flat land between the Atlantic Ocean and the Piedmont. p. 21.

Bethlehem (beth′ li hem). City in Lehigh and Northampton counties, on Lehigh River. (41°N/75°W). p. 153.

Blue Mountains (blü moun′ tənz). Range in southeastern Pennsylvania. Part of Appalachian Mountains. p. 171.

Braddock (brad′ ək). Town in Allegheny County, east of Pittsburgh. Has steel mills. (40°N/80°W). p. 25.

Brandywine Creek (bran′ dē wīn krēk). Flows south from Pennsylvania to Wilmington, Delaware. p. 65.

Bushy Run (bush′ ē rùn). Place in Westmoreland County where British defeated Indians in Pontiac's War. (40°N/80°W). p. 55.

Carlisle (kär līl′). Town in Cumberland County, west of Harrisburg. (40°N/77°W). p. 170.

Chadds Ford (chadz fôrd). Village in Delaware County, on Brandywine Creek. (40°N/76°W). p. 65.

Chambersburg (chām′ bèrz bèrg). Town in Franklin County. (40°N/78°W). p. 170.

Chester (ches′ tèr). City in Delaware County, on Delaware River. First settled by the Swedish. (40°N/75°W). p. 153.

Columbia (kə lum′ bē ə). Town in Lancaster County, on Susquehanna River. (40°N/76°W). p. 82.

Conestoga Valley (kän ə stō′ gə va′ lē). Valley southwest of Lancaster. Conestoga wagons were first made here. (40°N/76°W). p. 171.

Connellsville (kän′ əlz vil). City in Fayette County, north of Uniontown. (40°N/80°W). p. 171.

Cumberland (kum′ bèr lənd). City in western Maryland, on Potomac River. (40°N/79°W). p. 170.

Delaware Bay (del′ ə wär bā). Arm of Atlantic Ocean between Delaware and New Jersey. p. 44.

Delaware River (del′ ə wär riv′ ėr). River that forms the eastern boundary of Pennsylvania. Flows south into Atlantic Ocean at Delaware Bay. p. 21.

Devon (dev′ ən). A suburb west of Philadelphia. (40°N/75°W). p. 23.

Doylestown (doilz′ toun). Town in Bucks County, north of Philadelphia. (40°N/75°W). p. 170.

Easton (ēs′ tən). City in Northampton County, at joining of Lehigh and Delaware rivers. (41°N/75°W). p. 153.

Erie (ir′ ē). City in Erie County, in northwestern corner of Pennsylvania. Located on Lake Erie. (42°N/80°W). p. 22.

Erie Plain (ir′ ē plān). Low, almost flat land around Lake Erie. p 22.

Fort Bedford (fôrt bed′ fėrd). British fort where the town of Bedford, in Bedford County, is now. (40°N/78°W). p. 55.

Fort Casimir (fôrt kas′ ə mēr). Dutch fort on Delaware River where New Castle, Delaware, is now. (40°N/76°W). p. 44.

Fort Christina (fôrt kris tē′ nə). Swedish settlement on Delaware River where Wilmington, Delaware, is now. (40°N/76°W). p. 44.

Fort Duquesne (fôrt dü kān′). French fort where Pittsburgh is now. (40°N/80°W). p. 55.

Fort LeBoeuf (fôrt lə bəf′). French fort where Waterford, Erie County, is now. (42°N/80°W). p. 55.

Fort Ligonier (fôrt lig ə nir′). British fort where Ligonier, Westmoreland County, is now. (40°N/79°W). p. 55.

Fort Machault (fôrt mȧ shō′). French fort where Franklin, Venango County, is now. (41°N/80°W). p. 55.

Fort Necessity (fôrt ni ses′ ə tē). Fort built by George Washington in southwestern Pennsylvania at start of French and Indian War. (40°N/80°W). p. 55.

Fort Pitt (fôrt pit). British fort that replaced Fort Duquesne, where Pittsburgh is now. (40°N/80°W). p. 55.

Fort Presque Isle (fôrt pre skīl′). French fort where city of Erie is now. (42°N/80°W). p. 55.

Frankford (frangk′ fėrd). An area in the northeastern part of Philadelphia. (40°N/75°W). p. 83.

Franklin (frang′ klən). City in Venango County, in an area of oil and gas wells. (41°N/80°W). p. 153.

Germantown (jer′ mən toun). A section of Philadelphia first settled by German colonists. (40°N/75°W). p. 65.

Gettysburg (get′ ēz bėrg). Town in Adams County. Site of important battle in Civil War. (40°N/77°W). p. 170.

Gladwyne (glad′ win). A suburb west of Philadelphia. (40°N/75°W). p. 23.

Great Lakes (grāt lāks). Five large lakes in central North America: Superior, Michigan, Huron, Erie, Ontario. Drained by St. Lawrence River. p. 3.

Great Valley (grāt val′ ē). A wide valley on the southeastern side of the Ridge and Valley Region. p. 24.

Harrisburg (har′ əs bėrg). City in Dauphin County, on Susquehanna River. Capital of Pennsylvania. (40°N/77°W). p. 153.

Hazleton (hā′ zəl tən). City in Luzerne County, in coal-mining area. (41°N/76°W). p. 153.

Hollidaysburg (häl′ ə dāz bėrg). Town in Blair County, south of Altoona. (40°N/78°W). p. 82.

Indiana (in dē an′ ə). Town in Indiana County, northwest of Johnstown. (41°N/79°W). p. 170.

Johnstown (jäns′ toun). City in Cambria County, on Conemaugh River. Is in the bituminous coal-mining area. (40°N/79°W). p. 153.

Juniata River (jü nē at′ ə riv′ ėr). Flows east from Huntingdon County into Susquehanna River. p. 82.

Kittanning (kə tan′ ing). Town on Allegheny River, in Armstrong County. (41°N/80°W). p. 170.

Lake Erie (lāk ir′ ē). Located along boundary between Canada and United States. Second smallest of the Great Lakes. p. 22.

Lake Superior (lāk sủ pir′ ē ėr). Located along boundary between Canada and United States. Largest of the Great Lakes. p. 3.

Lancaster (lang′ kə stėr). City in Lancaster County, at the center of a rich farming area. (40°N/76°W). p. 153.

Lewistown (lü′ əs toun). Industrial town in Mifflin County, northwest of Harrisburg. (41°N/78°W). p. 170.

Mercersburg (mėr′ sėrz bėrg). Village in Franklin County. (40°N/78°W). p. 24.

Middletown (mid′ əl toun). Town in Dauphin County, on Susquehanna River, southeast of Harrisburg. (40°N/77°W). p. 170.

Mississippi River (mis ə sip′ ē riv′ ėr). Rises in Lake Itasca, Minnesota. Flows south through central United States to Gulf of Mexico in Louisiana. p. 3.

Monongahela River (mə nän gə hē lə riv′ ėr). Flows north and meets the Allegheny River to form the Ohio River at Pittsburgh. p. 25.

New Castle (nü′ kas əl). City in Lawrence County, western Pennsylvania, north of Pittsburgh. (41°N/80°W). p. 153.

New Gothenburg (nü gäth′ ən bėrg). Swedish settlement on Tinicum Island in Delaware River. First lasting, European settlement in what is now Pennsylvania. (40°N/75°W). p. 44.

Norristown (när′ əs toun). Town in Montgomery County, on Schuylkill River, northwest of Philadelphia. (40°N/75°W). p. 170.

Ohio River (ō hī ō riv′ ėr). Starts at joining of Allegheny and Monongahela rivers in Pittsburgh. Flows southwest into Mississippi River. p. 25.

Oil City (oil sit′ ē). City in Venango County, on Allegheny River. It has oil refineries. (41°N/80°W). p. 153.

Paoli (pā ō′ lē). A suburb west of Philadelphia. (40°N/75°W). p. 23.

Philadelphia (fil ə del′ fē ə). City in southeastern Pennsylvania. Located where Delaware and Schuylkill rivers join. Most populated city in the state. (40°N/75°W). p. 153.

Piedmont (pēd′ mänt). A region of low hills and wide valleys between the Atlantic Coastal Plain and the Appalachian Mountains. p. 23.

Pittsburgh (pits′ bėrg). City in southwestern Pennsylvania. Located where Allegheny and Monongahela rivers join and form the Ohio River. Second most populated city in the state. (40°N/80°W). p. 153.

Pocono Mountains (pō′ kə nō moun′ tənz). Range extending southwest from Pike County in northeastern Pennsylvania. p. 171.

Pottsville (päts′ vil). City in Schuylkill County, on upper Schuylkill River. (41°N/76°W). p. 171.

Raystown Lake (rāz′ toun lāk). Lake in Huntingdon County. p. 24.

Reading (red′ ing). Manufacturing city in Berks County, on Schuylkill River. (40°N/76°W). p. 153.

Ridge and Valley Region (rij and val′ ē rē′ jən). Mountain ranges separated by valleys, in central Pennsylvania. Part of Appalachian Mountains. p. 24.

Schuylkill River (skül′ kil riv′ ėr). Flows southeast into Delaware River at Philadelphia. p. 21.

Scranton (skran′ tən). City in Lackawanna County, in the anthracite coal-mining area. (42°N/76°W). p. 153.

Shillington (shil′ ing tən). Village in Berks County, southwest of Reading. (40°N/76°W). p. 23.

Springdale (spring′ dal). Village in Allegheny County, on Allegheny River, northeast of Pittsburgh. (41°N/80°W). p. 25.

State College (stāt kol′ ij). Town in Centre County, northwest of Lewistown. (41°N/78°W). p. 24.

Steelton (stēl′ tən). Town in Dauphin County, just south of Harrisburg. Has iron and steel mills. (40°N/77°W). p. 24.

Susquehanna River (səs kwə han′ ə riv′ ėr). River that flows mainly south through central Pennsylvania and into Chesapeake Bay. p. 5.

Titusville (tīt′ əs vil). City in Crawford County. Site of first oil well. (41°N/80°W). p. 170.

Trenton (tren′ tən). City on east side of Delaware River. Capital of New Jersey. (40°N/75°W). p. 170.

Uniontown (yün′ yən toun). City in Fayette County. (40°N/80°W). p. 170.

Upland (up′ lənd). Swedish settlement on Delaware River. Now part of Chester, Delaware County. (40°N/75°W). p. 44.

Upper Darby (up′ ėr där′ bē). Township in Delaware County, in urban area of Philadelphia. (40°N/75°W). p. 170.

Valley Forge (val′ ē fôrj). Place where Washington ·and his army spent a winter, northwest of Philadelphia. (40°N/75°W). p. 65.

Washington (wäsh′ ing tən). City in Washington County, southwest of Pittsburgh. (40°N/80°W). p. 170.

Wheeling (hwē′ ling). City in northern West Virginia, on Ohio River. (40°N/81°W). p. 170.

Wilkes-Barre (wilks′ bar ə). City in Luzerne County, on Susquehanna River. (41°N/76°W). p. 153.

Williamsport (wil′ yəmz pôrt). City in Lycoming County, on West Branch of Susquehanna River. (41°N/77°W). p. 153.

York (yôrk). City in York County, south of Harrisburg. (40°N/77°W). p. 153.

GLOSSARY

The page references tell where each entry appears in the text.

abolitionist (ab ə lish' ə nist).   A person who worked to end slavery in the United States. p. 94.

academy (ə kad' ə mē).   A school above an elementary school. p. 91.

acid rain (as' id   rān).   Rain or snow that has a high amount of certain acids due to air pollution. p. 161.

Allegheny Portage Railroad (al' ə gā' nē pôr' tij rāl' rōd').   A rail line, built in the late 1800s, that transported boats and barges to and from the Pennsylvania Canal through the Allegheny Mountains. p. 83.

alliance (a lī' əns).   An agreement among nations to unite to protect one another. p. 128.

Allies (al' īz).   The group, made up of the United Kingdom, France, the Soviet Union, the United States, and a number of other countries, that fought Germany, Italy, and Japan during World War II. p. 135.

anthracite (an' thrə sīt).   Hard coal. p. 15.

armistice (är' mə stis).   An agreement between countries to stop fighting each other. p. 129.

basic need (bā' sik   nēd).   Something that people need to live, such as a home, food, water, and clothing. p. 34.

bastions (bas' chənz).   Small towers of a fort, built at the points where the walls met. p. 57.

Bessemer process (bes' ə mər   präs' es).   A way of making steel by melting iron to burn out the impurities and change them into a gas. The gas then catches on fire and heats the iron even more — producing steel. This method of making steel was named after Henry Bessemer. p. 110.

bill (bil).   A possible law. p. 144.

biology (bī äl' ə jē).   The study of living things. p. 144.

bituminous (bə tü' mə nəs).   Soft coal. p. 14.

board of county commissioners (bôrd   uv   koun' tē kə mish' ə nərs).   A group of three people elected by the county's voters every 4 years. It is the board's job to make the laws for the county. p. 146.

borough (bur' ō).   A self-governing community or town. p. 146.

brittle (brit' əl).   Easily broken. p. 110.

canal (kə nal').   A waterway dug across land, for ships or small boats to travel through; it usually connects two waterways. p. 82.

candidate (kan' də dāt').   A person chosen by a group to run for an office. p. 101.

capital (kap' ə təl).   A place where the leaders of a settlement, state, or country work. p. 44.

capitol (kap' ə təl).   A building where state leaders met to make laws for Pennsylvania. p. 140.

celebrity (sə leb' rə tē).   A famous person. p. 164.

civil war (siv' əl   wôr).   A war between people of the same country; in America, the war between the North and the South, 1861–1865. p. 104.

clan (klan).   A group of families who have a common ancestor. p. 40.

climate (klī' mit).   The weather of a place over a long time. p. 9.

coke (kōk).   The fuel produced when bituminous coal is burned in large ovens. p. 86.

colony (kol' ə nē).   A place that is settled at a distance from the country that governs it. p. 47.

Conestoga wagon (kän' ə stō' gə wag' ən).   A wagon first used by the Pennsylvania Germans to carry their goods to Philadelphia; it was made of a canvas top that stretched over wooden hoops riding on four large, wooden wheels, and was pulled by six large horses. p. 54.

congress (kong' gris).   A meeting people have to discuss ideas or problems. p. 60.

congressional district (kən gresh' ə nəl   dis' trikt).   A division of the state, according to population. Each district elects one person to serve in the national House of Representatives. p. 148.

conservation (kän' sər vā' shən).   The preserving or protecting of natural resources. p. 131.

conservationist (kän sər vā' shə nəst).   A person who saves the environment and does not waste its gifts. p. 35.

constitution (kän stə tü' shən).   A set of laws by which a place is governed. p. 47.

Constitutional Convention (kän stə tü' shə nəl kən ven' shən).   The meeting in 1787, attended by representatives from the 13 United States, held to write a constitution. p. 71.

contemporary (kən tem' pə rer' ē).   In the style of the present or recent times. p. 163.

county (koun' tē).   The largest territorial division for local government within a state. p. 24.

176

county seat (koun′ tē sēt). The town or city where the county government is located. p. 146.

Declaration of Independence (dek lə rā′ shən uv in di pen′ dəns). A document explaining why the colonists were breaking away from Great Britain. p. 63.

depression (di presh′ ən). A time when many people do not have jobs. p. 133.

drift (drift). A mixture of sand, earth, rock, and stones carried by glaciers from one place to another. p. 18.

economy (i kän′ ə mē). How a state or country uses its workers and resources to produce goods and services. p. 132.

environment (en vī′ rən mənt). All the things around us, such as water, land, animals, plants, and air. p. 34.

Erie Triangle (ir′ ē trī′ ang əl). A piece of land shaped like a triangle that was claimed by the states of Massachusetts, New York, and Pennsylvania until 1792, when New York and Massachusetts gave up their claims and Pennsylvania bought the land from the United States. p. 72.

ethnic neighborhood (eth′ nik nā′ bər hood′). A place in which people from the same country or the same background live together. p. 121.

executive branch (eg zek′ yə tiv branch). The branch of government that carries out the laws. p. 143.

explorer (ek splôr′ ər). A person who looks for new things and new places. p. 42.

export (ek′ spôrt). Goods that are shipped out of a country. p. 152.

Fall Line (fôl līn). A line of small waterfalls and rapids. p. 20.

five-and-dime store (fīv ənd dīm stôr). A type of store that was started by Frank W. Woolworth in 1879 and that sold items for 5 and 10 cents. p. 118.

flax (flaks). A plant used to make linen cloth. p. 44.

fleet (flēt). A group of ships sailing together. p. 67.

Free School Act (frē skül′ akt). The act passed in Pennsylvania in 1834, whereby schools were free and every child could go to school; the beginning of public schools in Pennsylvania. p. 91.

frontier (frun tir′). Land that is on the edge of unsettled country. p. 67.

fuel (fü′ əl). Something that can be burned to make heat or power. p. 14.

General Assembly (jen′ ər əl ə sem′ blē). The name given to the legislative branch of government in Pennsylvania that is made up of two parts — the House of Representatives and the Senate. p. 143.

geography (jē og′ rə fē). The study of the earth and how people use it. p. 2.

glacier (glā′ sher). A thick sheet of ice. p. 18.

governor (guv′ ə nər). The most important leader of a settlement or state. p. 42.

grid (grid). A system of boxes on a map, formed by crossing latitude and longitude lines. p. 4.

gristmill (grist′ mil). A large building where wheat and other grains were ground into flour. p. 53.

hemp (hemp). A crop whose fibers are used to make very strong rope. p. 52.

heritage (her′ ət ij). The customs and beliefs handed down from one generation to the next. p. 121.

Hessian (hesh′ ən). A soldier from Germany who was hired by the British to fight in the American Revolution. p. 64.

historical fiction (his tôr′ ə kəl fik′ shən). A story that combines historical facts with imaginary people and events. p. 163.

history (his′ tər ē). The study of the past. p. 2.

House of Representatives (hous uv rep rə zen′ tə tivs). One part of the Pennsylvania General Assembly. Also the name of one part of our national Congress. p. 143.

humidity (hyü mid′ ə tē). The amount of moisture, or water, in the air. p. 8.

hydroelectric power (hī drō i lek′ trik pou′ ər). Electricity produced from moving water. p. 11.

immigrant (im′ ə grənt). A person who leaves his or her home in one country and moves to another country to live. p. 120.

import (im′ pôrt). Goods that are shipped into a country. p. 152.

judicial branch (jü dish′ əl branch). The branch of government that interprets, or explains, the laws. p. 144.

kerosene (ker′ ə sēn). A thin oil made from petroleum; used in lamps and stoves, to run farm machines, and as a fuel for jet planes. p. 87.

landfill (land fil'). A place that has long ditches and is covered with soil, where garbage and trash are buried. p. 161.

league (lēg). A group of people joined together for a common purpose. p. 33.

legislative branch (lej' is lā tiv branch). The branch of government that makes the laws. p. 143.

leisure time (lē' zhər tīm). Time spent away from work. p. 130.

Lenni-Lenape (le' nē len' ə pē). Original People – what the Delaware Indians called themselves. p. 32.

lieutenant governor (lü ten' ənt guv' ər nər). The person who takes over the duties of governor when the governor is not able to do the job. p. 143.

linsey-woolsey (lin' zē wül' zē). A cloth made from a mixture of linen and wool. p. 52.

literature (lit' ər ə chər). Writings of a certain time period that include novels, plays, and poetry. p. 163.

local government (lō' kəl guv' ərn mənt). The elected people who make and enforce the laws and provide public services in a county, city, or town. p. 140.

locomotive (lō kə mō' tiv). An engine that moves on its own power and is used to pull trains. p. 85.

longhouse (lông hous). A house built by the Iroquois Indians, in which a number of families lived. p. 36.

lubricant (lü' bri kənt). Something that helps machines run smoothly. p. 16.

maize (māz). Corn, planted by the earliest Indians, in Pennsylvania. p. 32.

mineral (min' ər əl). A substance, found in the earth, that is neither plant nor animal. p. 10.

moraine (mə rān'). A ridge formed by a drift. p. 18.

musical play (myü' zi kəl plā). A play in which actors and actresses sing most of their lines. p. 165.

natural boundary (nach' ər əl boun' dər ē). A boundary that exists in nature, such as a mountain range, river, or sea. p. 20.

natural resource (nach' ər əl ri sôrs'). A thing made by nature and is useful to people. p. 10.

neutral (nü' trəl). Not taking sides in an argument or fight. p. 135.

novel (näv' əl). A story with characters and a plot. p. 163.

open-hearth process (ō' pən härth präs' es). A way of making steel, whereby a bowl-shaped furnace is used to heat iron; the iron can be heated to higher temperatures in this kind of furnace. p. 114.

palisade (pal ə sād'). Fences of pointed logs the Iroquois Indians built around their villages to protect them from enemies and wild animals. p. 36.

patriot (pā' trē ət). A colonist who was against the unfair control of the colonies by Great Britain. p. 62.

pesticide (pes' tə sīd). A chemical used to kill certain insects. p. 160.

piedmont (pēd' mont). Land at the foot of the mountains. p. 23.

plain (plān). A strip of low, flat land that usually stretches from the ocean to the higher land farther inland. p. 20.

plantation (plan tā' shən). Large farm in the South. p. 94.

plateau (pla tō'). A raised, level piece of land that covers a large area. p. 25.

political boundary (pə lit' ə kel boun' der ē). A line made by people to separate one state or county from another. p. 2.

politics (päl' ə tiks). The art or science of guiding government. p. 100.

pollute (pə lut'). To make unclean. p. 131.

precipitation (pri sip ə tā' shən). The moisture that falls on the earth's surface in the form of rain, snow, sleet, hail, fog, or mist. p. 8.

prehistory (prē his' tə rē). The story of a people before they learned to write things down. p. 30.

Quaker (kwāk' ər). A member of the Society of Friends, a religious group that believes all people should live as friends and are equal in the eyes of God. p. 46.

ratify (rat' ə fī'). To approve or confirm. p. 71.

regiment (rej' ə mənt). A part of an army. p. 68.

region (rē' jən). An area of land whose parts have one or more common characteristics. p. 6.

repeal (ri pēl'). To take back. p. 60.

representative (rep ri zen' tə tiv). Someone people choose to speak for them. p. 62.

resort (ri zôrt'). A place where people go for recreation and entertainment. p. 155.

ridge (rij). A long strip of raised land formed by a drift. p. 18.

river system (riv′ ər sis′ təm). A group of streams and smaller rivers that flow into a big river. p. 10.

rural (roor′ əl). Having to do with the country, not the city. p. 134.

sachem (sā′ chəm). The Algonquian word for *chief*. p. 39.

secede (si sēd′). To formally withdraw from an organization or a nation. p. 102.

Secretary of State (sek′ rə ter ē uv stāt). The person responsible for keeping all official state records. p. 162.

Senate (sen′ it). A part of the General Assembly with 50 members, called senators. Also a name for a part of our national Congress. p. 143.

senator (sen′ ə tər). A member of the Senate, who represents the people in his or her senatorial district. A senator stays in office for 4 years. p. 143.

service industry (sėr′ vis in′ də strē). An industry that provides a service to people rather than goods. p. 152.

settlement (set′ əl mənt). The place where settlers live. p. 42.

settler (set′ lər). A person who moves to a new land to live. p. 42.

slavery (slā′ vər ē). The practice of one person owning another. p. 94.

Speaker of the House (spē′ kər uv the hous). The leading member of the House of Representatives. p. 163.

state (stāt). One of the 50 political divisions of the United States, each division having its own name and government. p. 2.

state government (stāt guv′ ərn mənt). The elected leaders who make and carry out the laws of a state. p. 140.

steamboat (stēm′ bōt). A boat moved by steam power. p. 84.

steel (stēl). A hard metal, stronger than iron. p. 110.

strike (strīk). To refuse to work until certain chánges are made. p. 116.

suburb (sub′ ərb). A smaller town or community near a large city. p. 138.

sweat lodge (swet′ läj). A special house where the Algonquian Indians took steam baths. p. 35.

temperature (tem′ pər ə chər). The amount of heat as measured on a given scale, such as the Fahrenheit scale or the Celsius scale. p. 8.

territory (ter′ ə tôr′ ē). An area of land. p. 101.

textile (teks′ təl). A woven fabric or cloth. p. 88.

toll (tōl). Money paid to use a road, to help pay for the building costs of the road and its care. p. 80.

township (toun′ ship). A division of a county, with its own local government. p. 146.

toxic waste (tok′ sik wāst). Dangerous chemicals and special products, from factories, that are buried or stored in the soil. p. 161.

transportation (trans pər tā′ shən). The moving of people and goods from one place to another. p. 80.

Treaty of Paris (tre′ tē uv par′ is). A peace treaty signed by the British and the Americans in 1783, ending the War for Independence. p. 70.

tribe (trīb). A group held together by family and social ties, geography, or custom. p. 32.

turnpike (tərn′ pīk). A new kind of road, built in the late 1700s in Pennsylvania, on which travelers had to pass through a turning gate, or pike. p. 80.

Underground Railroad (un′ dər ground′ rāl′ rōd′). A system of escape paths, formed by blacks and whites in the 1830s, to help slaves escape from the Southern slave states to the free states in the North. p. 97.

Union (yün′ yən). The states that did not secede from the United States. p. 104.

union (yün′ yən). A group of workers united to make their working conditions better. p. 89.

urban area (ėr′ bən ār′ ē ə). An area made up of a large city and its suburbs. p. 150.

veto (vē′ tō). To not approve a bill. p. 144.

wage (wāj). A payment of money for services. p. 126.

weather (′weTH ər). The way the air is at a certain time in a given place. p. 8.

Whiskey Rebellion (wis′ kē ri bel′ yən). A protest by a group of farmers, led by James McFarlane, against a tax placed on whiskey which they thought was unfair. President Washington sent in federal troops to end the rebellion in 1794. p. 74.

Woodland Indian (wood′ land in′ dē ən). An Indian of Pennsylvania whose home was in or near the woods. p. 32.

Workmen's Compensation Act (wėrk′ mənz käm′ pən sā′ shən akt). A law passed in 1915, whereby owners of industries had to pay some of the medical bills of workers injured while on the job. p. 128.

AVERAGE MONTHLY PRECIPITATION

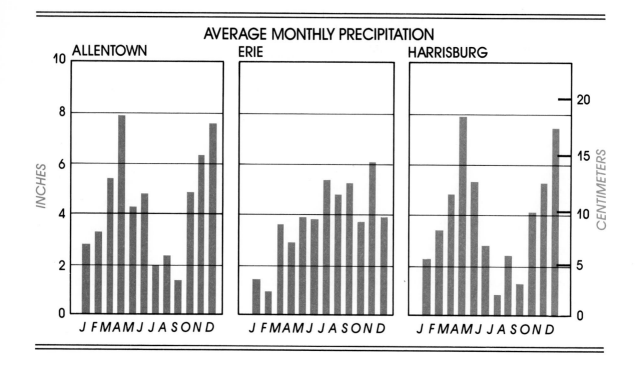

ALLENTOWN

ERIE

HARRISBURG

AVERAGE MONTHLY PRECIPITATION

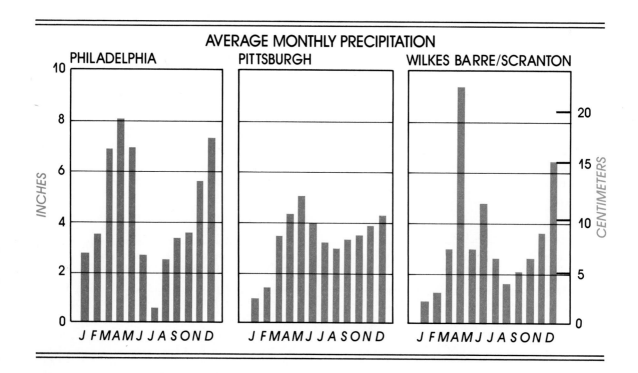

PHILADELPHIA

PITTSBURGH

WILKES BARRE/SCRANTON

AVERAGE MONTHLY TEMPERATURES

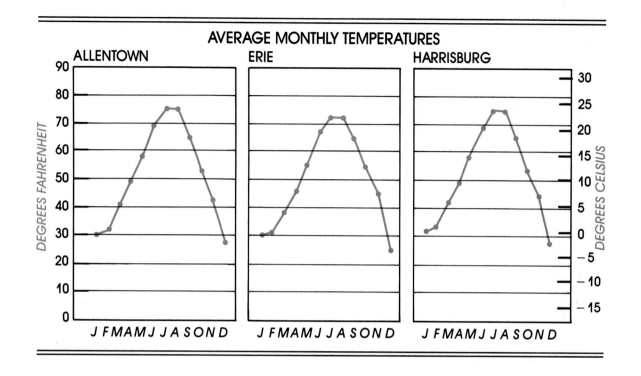

AVERAGE MONTHLY TEMPERATURES

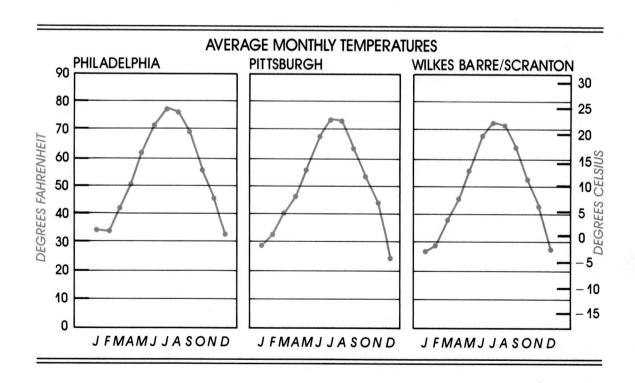

INDEX

CREDITS

Cover: Gene Ahrens
Unit Dividers and Front Matter Art: Neil Paulino
Illustrations: Peter Asprey; Yoshi Miyaki; Michele M. Epstein
Maps: R.R. Donnelley Cartographic Services

Time Lines: Michele M. Epstein

Chapter 1 3: Phill Degginger. 4: Shostal Associates. 7: *t.* Tom Tracey/The Stock Shop; *b.* Isaac Geib/Grant Heilman Photography. 10: Cary Wolinski/Stock, Boston. 11: Courtesy of Pennsylvania Power & Light. 12: *t.* deWys, Inc.; *b.* J. Irwin/H. Armstrong Roberts, Inc. 13: Grant Heilman Photography. 14: Pennsylvania Historical and Museum Commission. 15: *l.* Bob Hahn/Taurus Photos; *r.* Cary Wolinski/Stock, Boston.

Chapter 2 19: E.R. Degginger. 21: Robert Y. Richie/Shostal Associates. 22: Grant Heilman Photography. 23: J. Erwin/H. Armstrong Roberts, Inc. 24: Grant Heilman Photography. 25: Paul G. Wiegman/View Finder.

Chapter 3 31: Museum of the American Indian, The Heye Foundation. 34: Yale University Art Gallery, gift of de Lancey Koutze. 35: Courtesy of the American Museum of Natural History. 36: Historical Pictures Service, Chicago. 37: From the Ernest Smith Collection, Rochester Museum & Science Center, Rochester, N.Y. 39, 40: Museum of the American Indian, The Heye Foundation.

Chapter 4 43–45: Swedish Historical Society. 46: Historical Society of Pennsylvania, 47: The Granger Collection. 49: *t:* Courtesy of Pennsbury Manor; *b.* Pennsylvania Historical Society. 50: E.R. Degginger. 51: New York Public Library. 54: E.R. Degginger. 56–58: The Granger Collection. 59: Historical Pictures Service, Chicago.

Chapter 5 61: The Granger Collection. 63: J.L.G. Ferris Archives of 76 Bay Village, Ohio. 66: The Valley Forge Historical Society. 67: Culver Pictures. 68, 69: The Granger Collection. 70: Pennsylvania Historical & Museum Commission. 71: *t.* Independence National Historical Park Collection; *b.* Culver Pictures. 72: Independence National Historical Park Collection. 73: *t.* The Granger Collection; *b.* Bethlehem Steel. 74: The Granger Collection. 75: Irving S. Olds Collection, The New-York Historical Society. 76: National Museum of American Art, Smithsonian Institution, gift of Sulgrave Institution of the United States and Great Britain.

Chapter 6 81: Historical Pictures Service, Chicago. 83: Pennsylvania Historical & Museum Commission. 84–87: The Granger Collection. 88: The Bettmann Archive. 89: The Granger Collection. 90: Bucks County Historical Society, Mercer Museum. 91: Friends Historical Library, Swarthmore College. 92. *l.* Independence National Historical Park, Second Bank Collection; *r.* Silver Burdett.

Chapter 7 95: Historical Pictures Service, Chicago. 96: No credit. 97: Historical Pictures Service, Chicago. 98,99: The Granger Collection. 100: Courtesy of Mercersburg Academy. 101: The Granger Collection. 102: Anne S.K. Brown Military Collection, Brown University Library. 103: The Bettmann Archive. 104–106: The Granger Collection. 107: *l.* Historical Pictures Service, Chicago; *r.* The Granger Collection. 108: The Granger Collection.

Chapter 8 111: The Granger Collection. 112: The Bettmann Archive. 114: Carnegie Library, Pittsburgh. 115: Historical Pictures Service, Chicago. 116, 117: The Granger Collection. 118: *t.l.* Bettmann Archive; *t.r.* Courtesy of H.J. Heinz, Co.; *b.* courtesy of F.W. Woolworth, Co. 119: The Bettmann Archive. 120: The Granger Collection. 121: Applegate Collection, Balch Institute for Ethnic Studies 122: Andrew Sacks/Black Star.

Chapter 9 127: Historical Pictures Service, Chicago. 128, 129: The Bettmann Archive. 130: Culver Pictures. 131: Brown Brothers. 132: *l.* Brown Brothers; *r.* Camerique. 133: Culver Pictures. 134: UPI/Bettmann Newsphotos. 135: *American Heritage*, Collection of the Navy's Combat Art Paintings. 136: The Bettmann Archive. 137: UPI/Bettmann Newsphotos. 138, 139: Michael Provost for Silver Burdett.

Chapter 10 141: Dave Farmerie/Viewfinder. 142: *l.* Pennsylvania Historical & Museum Commission; *r.* Courtesy Governor's Office, Commonwealth of Pennsylvania. 143: Allied Pix. 144: Photo by Bachrach, courtesy of the Supreme Court of Pennsylvania. 147: Sal di Marco, Jr./Black Star. 148: Dennis Brack/Black Star.

Chapter 11 151: Camerique. 152: Michael Provost for Silver Burdett. 154: Photo by Herwig G. Schultzer, courtesy of Donnelley. 155: *l.* Photo by Gregory M. Fota, courtesy of Moravian College; *r.* Camerique. 156: Courtesy of Pennsylvania State University. 157: Carnegie Museum of Natural History, Carnegie Institute. 158: *l.* Pennsylvania Chamber of Commerce; *r.* Erie-Western Pennsylvania Port Authority. 159: L.L.T. Rhodes/Taurus Photos. 160: Erich Hartmann/Magnum, Rachel Carson Council, Inc. 161: William Felger/Grant Heilman Photography. 162: UPI/Bettmann Newsphotos. 163: E.R. Degginger. 165: Warring Abbott. 166: Focus on Sports. 167: Peter Byron for Silver Burdett.

C D E F G H I J—VH—96 95 94 93 92 91